LENIN'S
LAST
STRUGGLE

ANN ARBOR PAPERBACKS FOR THE STUDY OF
RUSSIAN AND SOVIET HISTORY AND POLITICS

Ronald Grigor Suny, Series Editor

The series publishes classic and out-of-print works
in Russian history and politics, presenting them with
new prefaces in which prominent experts assess the books'
continued importance to the field and make their value clear
to a new generation of students and scholars. The works to be
included will span the entire period of modern Russian and
Soviet history and demonstrate the variety of approaches
and interpretations that have long made the study of
Russia's past an integral part of our
understanding of ourselves.

Karamzin's Memoir on Ancient and Modern Russia
Richard Pipes

Lenin's Last Struggle
Moshe Lewin

LENIN'S
LAST
STRUGGLE

MOSHE LEWIN

TRANSLATED BY
A. M. SHERIDAN SMITH

With a New Introduction

THE UNIVERSITY OF MICHIGAN PRESS

Ann Arbor

Copyright © by the University of Michigan 2005
Translation of *Le dernier combat de Lénine.* First published
in 1968 by Random House under the Pantheon Books imprint,
and reprinted by Monthly Review Press, 1978.
Published in the United States of America by
The University of Michigan Press
Printed and bound by CPI Group (UK) Ltd, Croydon, CR0 4YY
♾

2008   2007   2006   2005   4   3   2   1

A CIP catalog record for this book is available from the British Library.

Library of Congress Cataloging-in-Publication Data

Lewin, Moshe, 1921–
    [Dernier combat de Lénine. English]
    Lenin's last struggle / Moshé Lewin ; translated by A.M. Sheridan Smith,
with a new introduction.
        p. cm.
    Includes bibliographical references and index.
    ISBN 978-0-472-03052-1 (pbk. : alk. paper)
    1. Soviet Union—Politics and government—1917–1936. 2. Lenin, Vladimir
Il'ich, 1870–1924. I. Title.

    DK266.5.L4513 2005
    947.084'1'092—dc22   2004065834

ISBN13 978-0-472-03052-1 (paper)
ISBN13 978-0-472-02667-8 (electronic)

The worst thing that can befall the leader of an extreme party is to be compelled to take over a government in an epoch when the movement is not yet ripe for the domination of the class which he represents, and for the realization of the measures which that domination implies. . . . Thus he necessarily finds himself in an insolvable dilemma. What he can *do contradicts all his previous actions, principles and immediate interests of his party, and what he* ought *to do cannot be done. . . . Whoever is put into this awkward position is irrevocably doomed.*

—F. ENGELS, *The Peasant War in Germany*

Those Communists are doomed who imagine that it is possible to finish such an epoch-making undertaking as completing the foundations of socialist economy (particularly in a small-peasant country) without making mistakes, without retreats, without numerous alterations to what is unfinished or wrongly done. Communists who have no illusions, who do not give way to despondency, and who preserve their strength and flexibility "to begin from the beginning" over and over again in approaching an extremely difficult task, are not doomed (and in all probability will not perish).

—V. I. LENIN, "Notes of a Publicist"

CONTENTS

PREFACE

A considerable number of left-wing dictatorships have appeared on the international political scene since World War II, the only precedent for states of this type being the Soviet Union, which is now celebrating its fiftieth anniversary. These fifty years of socialist experience could no doubt be very useful to the new states if they took the trouble to acquire a thorough knowledge of them and to reflect on the vicissitudes of the first proletarian dictatorship. Thus the failure of the "agroindustrial combines" created in the USSR in 1929–1930 foreshadowed that of the communes of the People's China, and Nikita Khrushchev was a victim of the same megalomania when he tried to launch his *agrogoroda* in 1950. However, apart from a small number of Soviet writers, it is largely the English-speaking specialists who have pointed out how singularly rich in economic and social lessons is the period of the New Economic Policy, and it is they who have least to gain from such knowledge. Many other periods and other aspects of Soviet history remain, to a greater or lesser degree, in obscurity, illuminated here and there by the researches of a few scholars. It is unlikely that the governing elite of the USSR knows the history of its country—apart from what each individual has experienced at first hand—

for Marxist countries, for some peculiar reason, tend to treat their history as a state secret. The leaders seem to believe that knowledge of an often tragic past acts as a discouragement for those whose duty it is to build the future; whereas in fact ignorance of history destroys any forward-looking attitude far more surely than its divulgence and analysis. But as long as history can be publicized only with official permission it will remain obscure, for it is the scientific discipline most likely to be vitiated by state monopoly.

This study of Lenin and of his thought during his last year is not, of course, entirely new. A good deal was learned on this subject from Trotsky's revelations in the 1920s, and again from the repercussions of the affair of Lenin's "testament," set in train by the Twentieth Congress of the CPSU. But recent Soviet publications have enabled us to take up this subject again and to attempt a more accurate and more detailed reconstruction of the relations that emerged among the top Party leaders at the time of Lenin's illness. We hope at the same time to extend the analysis of Lenin's "testament," that is, of his political thinking during this last period, and to offer on occasion a new interpretation of it.

Among the documents from which our source material has been taken, three are of exceptional importance: first, the latest edition of Lenin's *Works*—the fifth edition—not only more complete than previous ones but accompanied by an important body of notes and commentary; second, the memoirs of Fotieva, one of Lenin's personal secretaries; and third, the "Journal of Lenin's Secretaries," working notes made between November 21, 1922, and March 6, 1923, and published for the first time in 1963 by a Soviet historical review.[1] These notes are as important in content as they are

[1] *Voprosy Istorii,* No. 2, 1963. The "Journal" is also reproduced in V. I. Lenin, *Sochineniya* (Works), 5th ed. (Moscow, Institute of Marxism-Leninism, 1958–65), Vol. XLV, pp. 455–86.

peculiar in form. They are in the form of a four-columned notebook showing the date, the secretary's name, instructions given, and notes on how they were carried out; the last column also contains notes on the day's events in the office of the chairman of the Sovnarkom, the Council of People's Commissars. Accounts are given, sometimes day by day, of the chairman's appointments, his correspondence, and even his slightest actions and gestures. This information is enlightening as to Lenin's working methods, but at the outset it provides no particularly startling revelation. It soon becomes obvious, however, that Lenin is slowing down the pace of his work; he no longer comes to his office regularly, but often prefers to send for one of the secretaries and dictate in his private apartment. His health was already failing and his doctors had ordered him to work less, to take frequent rests in the country, and to miss certain meetings of the Council of Commissars or of the Politburo. On December 13, 1922, the day after an important meeting with Dzerzhinsky, Lenin had two serious attacks and was forced at last to obey the orders of his doctors to postpone his work and take to his bed. At this point the "Journal" begins to be quite fascinating. When Lenin sends for his secretaries, in order to give them instructions or to dictate, they observe him with scrupulous attention, and hang on his every word and movement, which they note down in the "Journal." Lenin was confined to his bed in a small room of his Kremlin apartment, his right hand and right leg paralyzed, almost completely isolated from the outside world and, apparently, cut off from all government activity. The doctors' orders were strict on this matter and they were reinforced by a decision of the Politburo.

But however fragmentary the notes of the "Journal" may be, they are enough to show the intense and passionate struggle that Lenin, paralyzed and no doubt aware of his ap-

proaching end, was waging not only against physical decline
but also against the leadership of his party. With great effort
he drew up a comprehensive survey of the situation of the
country, worked out a program of action, and tried hard to
persuade his colleagues on the Politburo and the Central
Committee to accept it. This program, which was not re-
quested by the members of the Politburo, involved considerable changes in government methods, in personnel, and to
some extent in objectives. The majority of the Politburo were
unenthusiastic.

With the help only of a few women—Krupskaya, his wife,
Maria Ilinichna, his sister, and three or four secretaries,
notably Fotieva and Volodicheva—Lenin fought obstinately
to get hold of the dossiers he needed. He spoke to influential
members and suggested specific lines of action; he sought
allies and sounded out the opinions of various leaders, by
indirect means if necessary; he worked on a lengthy report
for the next Party Congress and published articles, for he
finally managed to obtain the permission either of his doctors
or of the Politburo itself to continue with some of his activities. But there were other activities that he pursued in secret
—and with good reason. With the help of his closest friends,
Lenin was engaged in nothing less than a plot to ensure the
future success of his life's work. The center of the "conspiracy"—the word is Lenin's own—consisted of a private
commission that he had secretly formed to inquire into
certain events in Georgia in which leading figures in the
Party had been implicated. The circumstances of this affair,
which the "Journal" enables us to reconstruct in detail, reveal
or confirm what were the personal and political relations of
the three leaders, Lenin, Trotsky and Stalin. The notes also
give us some idea of the physical and mental effort expended
by a man as seriously ill as Lenin was; they help us to feel

his presence, the intensity of his feelings, the power of his personality, the charm of his laughter.

But at this point we are confronted by something that goes well beyond autobiographical trivia. Historians have often spoken of an "intellectual crisis" that Lenin may have experienced during this final period, of a "*coup d'état*" that he was preparing, of a revolt against the results of his own work, and of the tragedy of a great revolutionary who thought he could see his ideal of emancipating the masses disappearing before his eyes and who felt that he was losing all control of events because of the unfortunate coincidence of an accident in his physical life and implacable political realities. In the course of this study we shall have occasion to re-examine these postulates.

But the situation in which the Soviet regime found itself during Lenin's illness and the problems that confronted Lenin in his last months are still relevant to the world today. Consequently, we shall find ourselves confronted with issues that go beyond the scope of a biography. Lenin wanted to give the regime he had helped to establish an adequate socio-economic framework and to create methods of management that would be adaptable both to this framework and to the ultimate aims of the Revolution; the result was the NEP, the New Economic Policy. He tried to impart a new style, vigor and efficacy to the dictatorial machine. His behavior poses the problem of the duties and responsibilities incumbent on the leaders of a dictatorship that claims to be socialist. These three key questions are always interdependent during the earliest stages of a regime of the Soviet type and of a dictatorship that sets out to develop a backward country.

The first question, as it presented itself to Lenin, concerns the balance to be struck between the spontaneous forces necessary to the launching of the economy, namely the peas-

ant smallholders, artisans and businessmen, and the centralized, state-owned and more or less planned sector that
must give the economy as a whole the general direction required. Under the NEP, this was already the dilemma of the
"market" and the "plan." Even today, despite the disappear-
ance of the peasant smallholders and of the middle classes of
a capitalist type, it is still one of the major problems pre-
occupying the minds of the Soviet leaders, who are discover-
ing that the two notions are not mutually exclusive, but
complementary if they can be implemented simultaneously
in a harmonious fashion.

The second question, that of the functioning of the dictatorial state, will require more of our attention. In the beginning the dictatorship is organized with the aim of ac-
complishing its mission of developing the country and
establishing a greater degree of social justice—the principles
for which the revolution was fought. But the dictatorial state
tends to become a rigid organism with its own laws and
interests; it may become a mere distortion of its original purpose; it may escape the control of its founders and disappoint,
for a long time at least, the hopes of the masses. The instrument then becomes an end in itself. A coercive system set up
to promote freedom may, instead of providing the social
forces outside the state machine with an increasing share of
power, become a machine of oppression. Every state that
tries to carry out in an efficient way difficult tasks that are
often unpleasant for the masses inevitably creates a privileged
body of cadres who enjoy a certain prestige and material and
political advantages. If these privileges are not controlled
and kept within strict limits by social and economic realities,
they soon become dangerous and impede development.

There is always a risk that men will become corrupted by
power and privilege. The leaders and administrators of the

state that has emerged from a revolution, even if they belong to the often courageous, idealistic and dedicated elite that made the revolution, are tempted to attach more value to their privileges than to the function that justifies them— especially if they are isolated among a mass of new administrators who are of neither the level nor the value of the founders. How then can decline be avoided and the purity of the revolution be preserved? There is no easy answer. All that can be said is that the moral level and political consciousness of the elite, together with certain institutional guarantees, are positive factors. In these conditions it is all the more valuable to remember Lenin's injunction to Communists to retain "strength and flexibility" and to be always ready "to go back to the beginning"; they must not lose their critical spirit and must be willing, if necessary, to rebuild all or much of what has been attempted.

No more will be said of the implications of these questions for the present day. After drawing attention to them here, we shall merely try as objectively as possible to provide the material required for such a reflection, as it comes out of Lenin's last struggle.

GLOSSARY
OF RUSSIAN TERMS

In cases where it is difficult to find an exact equivalent in English, a number of Russian terms have been used in this book. Here is a short list of them.

Administrirovanie: a system of management based on coercive measures, used by the bureaucracy

Apparatchik (pl. *apparatchiki*): functionary of the Communist Party apparatus

Cheka (*Chrezvychainaya Komissiya*): Extraordinary Commission, the Soviet political police (1917–1922), operating against counterrevolutionary activities

Chinovnik (pl. *chinovniki*): bureaucrat, in a pejorative sense; *chinovnichestvo:* bureaucracy

Dzerzhimorda (pl. *dzerzhimordy*): literally, he who holds you by the muzzle; the nickname for the Tsarist police

Edinonachalie: Russian term for monocratic rule by directors or other senior administrators

Gensek (*Generalnyi Sekretar*): General Secretary of the Party's Central Committee (CC), leader of its secretariat

Gosplan: State Planning Commission

Kavburo: Caucasian Bureau of the Party

Kombedy (*Komitety Bednoty*): Committees of Poor Peasants, village organizations during the civil war

Kulturnichestvo: the promotion of culture in the widest sense

Nepman (pl. *nepmany*): beneficiary of the NEP (New Economic Policy), a member of the new bourgeoisie

Nezavisimets (pl. *nezavisimtsy*): a supporter of *nezavisimost,* national independence

Orgburo: Organization Bureau; its membership was elected by the Central Committee; its function was to deal with problems referred to it by the Politburo and to coordinate organizational problems under the Politburo's guidance

Politburo: Political Bureau, the highest political organ in the Party and the state; members were elected by the CC; at the period of Lenin's illness there were seven members and four deputies

RKI (*Raboche-Krestyanskaya Inspektsiya*): Workers' and Peasants' Inspection, the commissariat charged with the control of the state administration; it worked in tandem with the CCC

RSFSR: the Russian Socialist Federal Soviet Republic

Secretariat: composed of secretaries of the CC, who were elected by the TSKK and its apparatus; created for executing current organizational work of the Party and for guiding the apparatus

Sovkhoz (pl. *sovkhozy*): state farm

Sovnarkom (*Soviet Narodnykh Komissarov*): Council of People's Commissars, sometimes abbr. SNK

STO (*Soviet Truda i Oborony*): Council of Labor and Defense, a committee of the SNK, charged with implementation and coordination of policy in the fields of economics and defense

Tsekist (pl. *tsekisty*): member of the Central Committee (*Tseka*)

TSKK (*Tsentralnya Kontrolnaya Komissiya*): the Party's Central Control Commission (abbr. CCC in this book)

Uchraspred (*Uchetno-Raspredelitel'nyi Otdel*): Records and Assignments Department

Velikoderzhavnik (pl. *velikoderzhavniki*): supporter of a Great Power policy, imperialist, chauvinist

VSNKH (*Vysshi Soviet Narodnogo Khozyaistva*): Supreme Council of National Economy

VTSIK (*Vserossiskii Tsentral'nyi Ispolnitel'nyi Komitet*): All-Russian Central Executive Committee

Zakkraykom (*Zakavkazsky Kraevoy Komitet*): Party Committee in the Transcaucasian Federation, grouping the Republics of Georgia, Azerbaijan, and Armenia

CHRONOLOGY
OF
EVENTS

EARLY SUMMER 1918– DECEMBER 1920   Civil war (and period of "war communism").

1921

MARCH   New Economic Policy proclaimed (grain requisition replaced by a tax, first in kind, later in money).

DECEMBER   Lenin sick.

1922

JANUARY– FEBRUARY   Lenin gets additional six weeks vacation from the Politburo because of his illness.

MARCH 3   First letter to Kamenev against any weakening of the state's monopoly of foreign trade.

MARCH 6– MARCH 25   A new long vacation because of poor health.

MARCH 27– APRIL 2   Eleventh Party Congress.

APRIL 23   Operation to extract from Lenin's body one of the two bullets fired at him in August 1918 by the Social Revolutionary Fanya Kaplan.

MAY 15   Letter to Stalin suggesting a decision of the Politburo to reconfirm as inalterable the principle of state monopoly of foreign trade. Stalin resists.

MAY 22   Politburo accepts Lenin's demands concerning foreign trade monopoly.

MAY 25   Lenin partly paralyzed and loses ability to speak.

MIDDLE OF JUNE   Lenin's health improves.

AUGUST 10   Decision to convene a commission on relations among the Soviet Republics.

AUGUST 11   Commission works on and adopts Stalin's "autonomization" project.

AUGUST 21   Lenin talks with Stalin about the RKI and the next day writes a letter to RKI leaders criticizing the work of this institution.

SEPTEMBER 15 Stalin's project bluntly rejected by the Georgian Central Committee.

SEPTEMBER 22 Lenin asks Stalin to keep him informed about the decisions concerning relations among the Republics.

SEPTEMBER 24–25 Stalin's commission reconvenes and adopts Stalin's "autonomization" project in a more definite version.

SEPTEMBER 25 The dossier on the commission's work transmitted by Stalin to Lenin.

SEPTEMBER 26 Lenin invites Stalin for a talk on the unification of the Republics.

Lenin writes to Kamenev proposing his own version: the creation of the USSR.

SEPTEMBER 27   Lenin receives Mdivani for a talk on the unification project.

Stalin, in a letter to Politburo members, accuses Lenin of "national liberalism."

SEPTEMBER 28–30   Lenin meets separately with Ordzhonikidze, three members of the Georgian CC, and Myasnikov from Azerbaijan, to discuss the unification problems.

OCTOBER 2   Lenin back from Gorki and working in the Kremlin.

OCTOBER 6   The Politburo session (Lenin absent) decides to limit the state's foreign trade monopoly; Lenin's USSR project adopted; Lenin writes to Kamenev that he is going to fight Great Russian chauvinism.

OCTOBER 11   Lenin meets Trotsky. They discuss the monopoly problem and common fight against bureaucracy.

OCTOBER 13   Letter to Stalin criticizing decision on foreign trade and asking for it to be revised.

OCTOBER 21   Lenin assails the Georgians for their refusal to accept the Transcaucasian Federation.

OCTOBER 22   The Georgian CC resigns collectively.

NOVEMBER   Numerous complaints from Georgia to
(FIRST PART)   Moscow against Ordzhonikidze.

Tsintsadze's letter reaches Lenin and arouses his suspicions against the Stalin-Ordzhonikidze line in Georgia.

NOVEMBER 5–   The Fourth Congress of the Comintern in
DECEMBER 5   Moscow.

NOVEMBER 13   Lenin's speech at the Fourth Comintern
                 Congress.

NOVEMBER 20   Lenin's last public speech (at the session
                 of the Moscow Soviet).

NOVEMBER 24   Lenin, suspicious, abstains from voting on
                 the composition of the investigation
                 commission on the Georgian affair.

NOVEMBER 25   Politburo approves the composition of this
                 commission under Dzerzhinsky; the
                 commission leaves for Tbilisi.

END OF   "The incident": Ordzhonikidze strikes
NOVEMBER   Kabanidze, Mdivani's supporter.

DECEMBER 7–12   Lenin on leave in Gorki.

DECEMBER 9   Rykov comes back from Georgia, sees
                 Lenin.

DECEMBER 12   Proposition to Trotsky to defend, at the
                 next CC session, their common opinions
                 on the foreign trade monopoly.

DECEMBER 12–15   Exchange of letters between Lenin and
                 Trotsky on Lenin's proposition and
                 Trotsky's suggestions.

DECEMBER 13   Lenin suffers two dangerous strokes.

DECEMBER 15   Lenin writes to Stalin that he "has taken
                 the necessary steps to retire" and that he
                 has concluded an agreement with Trot-
                 sky, who will defend their common posi-
                 tion on the foreign trade monopoly.

DECEMBER 18   CC session rescinds previous decision and
                 reaffirms adoption of the Lenin-Trotsky
                 position on foreign trade; CC makes Sta-

	lin responsible for Lenin's medical supervision.
DECEMBER 21	Lenin's brief letter congratulating Trotsky on the victory at the CC session.
DECEMBER 22	Stalin assails Krupskaya for having written letter dictated by Lenin.
NIGHT OF DECEMBER 22–23	Lenin again half paralyzed.
DECEMBER 23	Lenin asks his doctors' permission to dictate some notes.
DECEMBER 24	Lenin says he will refuse to be treated by his doctors if he is not permitted to dictate his "journal." Permission is granted by the Politburo.
DECEMBER 23–31	Lenin dictates his notes, known as his "Testament." The memorandum on the national question and the Georgian affair, dictated on December 30–31, is the last of these notes, with a subsequent addition on Stalin.
DECEMBER 30	The first Congress of Soviets proclaims the creation of the USSR.

1923

JANUARY–FEBRUARY	Lenin dictates five articles: "Pages from a Journal," "On Cooperation," "Our Revolution," "On the Workers' and Peasants' Inspection," and "Better Fewer, But Better."
JANUARY 4	Lenin adds to his "Testament" a proposition to demote Stalin.
JANUARY 24	Lenin asks for the dossiers of the Dzerzhinsky commission findings. The Politburo is reluctant.

JANUARY 25   The Politburo session endorses the con-
              clusions of the Dzerzhinsky commission
              on the Georgian affair which white-
              washes Ordzhonikidze and condemns
              Mdivani and the Georgian CC.

FEBRUARY 1   The Politburo yields to Lenin's demand
              and turns over to him the commission's
              papers. Lenin asks his secretaries to
              study the material and gives instructions
              how to do it.

MARCH 3   Lenin's private investigation committee
              submits to him its findings on the
              Georgian affair.

MARCH 5   Letter to Trotsky asking him to take up,
              in both their names, the defense of the
              Georgian CC at the CC session. Trotsky
              answers the same day. Lenin begins
              dictating a letter to Stalin.

MARCH 6   Lenin finishes a letter to Stalin demanding
              that he apologize for his rude treatment
              of Krupskaya. Another letter to the
              Georgians, Mdivani and his friends, an-
              nouncing that Lenin is on their side
              against Stalin and Ordzhonikidze.
              Kamenev hears from Krupskaya that
              Lenin intends to crush Stalin politically.
              Lenin's health worsens critically.

MARCH 10   A new stroke paralyzes half of Lenin's
              body and deprives him of his capacity to
              speak. Lenin's political activity is fin-
              ished.

1924

JANUARY 21   Lenin's death.

THE LENIN-STALIN IMBROGLIO
Introduction to the New Edition

The past century cannot be understood without dwelling on its monumental failings—its economic crises, its two world wars, its inability to confront the growing world pool of poverty. These circumstances include the downfall of the Tsarist regime and the appearance of a quite new and enigmatic creature—the USSR—with its unexpected and unpredictable rise and its latter-day, rather more predictable, downfall. Materials from (partly) open Russian archives have allowed a "return to history" by parties like Mensheviks, Socialist-Revolutionaries, Liberals—parties that were previously banned by the Soviet regime. But it is less often realized that in fact the history of the Bolsheviks remains poorly known, and the Bolshevik leader, V. I. Lenin, continues to attract curiously many detractors who serve ideologies rather than our need to understand events of great complexity. There is also a quite amusing tendency to dig up personal features of Lenin, his outbursts of anger and other episodes that might have occurred when a tense, sometimes choleric Lenin was immersed in situations and actions demanding the utmost concentration on the mounting tasks at hand—not to mention feeling the effects of two bullets lodged in his body by a political opponent.

The key to his personality and the essence of his "ism" are to understand that Lenin's main role was that of a political strategist acting in extremely confusing and dramatic circumstances. The strategies in question can be understood only by reconstructing the historical landscape in which he was immersed. The key feature that requires the historian's attention is that of concatenated crises—the one crisis afflicting the West (where Lenin and many of the Bolshevik top leaders lived); the other, correlated but different, that undermined the Tsarist empire where the bulk of the Russian Social Democrats lived and acted in conditions of conspiracy and in a constant battle with the Tsarist police, whose secret agents also penetrated their organizations abroad. In the West they experienced the devastating effects of the decomposition of the Second International; in Russia they shared the agonies of a crumbling political system, unable, notably, to run a war machine and suffering defeats and colossal human losses that further undermined the enfeebled sociopolitical system. The year 1917 was yet another chapter for political strategy to cope with—mainly the growing decomposition of the country, where governments changed every two months, government control over events was waning, and what was looming ahead was obviously nothing less than a national calamity. The key players in these circumstances would have to face not just a "crisis" but an interconnected chain of crises, in part "imported" from abroad, in part emerging from the chaos of an unhinged country. The Bolsheviks stepped into a morass that nobody else could face—and a new system emerged that allowed the country to survive. The debates about these events never stopped.

After Lenin died he was replaced by Stalin, and soon one of the most tenacious of the propagandist labels began to be heard, becoming in many quarters almost a canon of faith, namely, that Lenin and Bolshevism begot Stalin and Stalinism—an easy-to-remember simplifier that seems to explain everything when in fact it has nothing to do with a reality that is so much more complicated and, let us add, more interesting. If this claim was true, why did Stalin work so hard to actually physically destroy most of the Bolshevik cadres? It was little known and seldom noticed that the relationship between Lenin and Stalin during Lenin's last two years was not just tense, it was characterized by hostility so profound that only Lenin's physical decline prevented him from demoting Stalin from his post as Secretary General, if not expelling him from the party altogether. The two men became almost open political enemies, and this was why anyone who might have known this—in fact, the whole Bolshevik organization—was exterminated and there was no need to speak seriously about a political party at all. In conditions of personal despotism, where decisions are made by one man and the apparatus puts them into effect, a political party is a red herring.

It is true that Stalin initially used terms such as "Bolshevism" and "Leninism" to legitimize his power, but a little homework can show that this was a calculated masquerade. Stalin worked hard, in fact, to eliminate ideologically and physically both Bolshevism as a political party and Leninism as its guiding strategic orientation. He did not follow even one of the ideas that became known as Lenin's "Testament." Instead he followed a path that was his own from the very beginning of the revolutionary era—maybe even much earlier—leading him finally to the adoption of a version of the old Russian autocracy, served with a nationalistic ideology hailing directly from an ancient historical tradition.

All this means that rather than "continuing" Lenin, a phenomenon such as Stalinism had its own roots in the tradition of a country still basically mired in the preurban stage economically, culturally, and socially. With many believing that nothing but a despotic state and a cultic ruler can control such a society, we can safely conclude that Stalin was no accident in the Russian conditions of the day and that probably there was little in common between Stalin and Bolshevism well before the Revolution.

Bolsheviks (the party) and Leninism (its political strategy) were no accidents either. They initially won thanks to a capacity to correctly diagnose the character of the crises the country was facing and skill and audacity in executing the power takeover and defending it successfully through a bloody civil war. This success was based on their ability to transform a swelling peasant *jacquerie* into a plebeian revolution, where many peasants were enrolled in the Red Army and many others, even if they did not support—or even fought—the Bolsheviks, massively refused support for the Whites. The ability to both unleash and tame a massive outpouring of rural violence showed that the Bolsheviks possessed an unexpected state-building capacity that convinced, symptomatically, many of the previously monarchist Russian generals and lesser ranks that the Bolsheviks were more serious than any other contender and that they could save the country.

Without expanding on a subject that demands lengthy explanations, we can just restate that both the emerging Stalinism and the initially victorious Bolsheviks were separate political phenomena that had their roots in the Russian political soil. We know who won and what followed.

But let us now sum up what "Bolshevism"—as represented by Lenin—was about. During the period when Lenin's conflict with Stalin was deepening, especially dur-

ing the battle over what kind of status non-Russian nationals
would receive in the USSR (which then was in the process of
being created), Lenin, who was already ill but amazingly
alert intellectually, proposed his program of state building
that postulated the following: (1) abandoning the unrealistic
socialist vision and aiming instead at "state capitalism" and
a market economy that the country badly needed; (2) making, so to speak, a political pact with the peasantry—then the
bulk of the population—promoting development of a free,
rural cooperative movement and refraining—he under-
lined—from any compulsion, any "communism," in the
countryside; (3) organizing the workings of the Party in a
way in which members—many of them workers—could
exercise a say in Party politics, controlling the top—especially the Secretary General—and ensuring that Party congresses and other bodies remained potent; (4) allowing non-
Russian nationals (most of them rural populations, too) to
enjoy statehood and equality of rights with the Russian
majority—Lenin insisted in particular on fighting against the
still-powerful Russian nationalism that could ruin the whole
edifice.

Considering that none of this was adopted by Stalin, we
had better dump the useless clichés and consider whether
and to what extent some of the Leninist program and other
Soviet developments could still be of value in a world where
backward, still-rural countries are living in misery and are
commanded by inept, oppressive regimes.

LENIN'S
LAST
STRUGGLE

1

A
DICTATORSHIP
IN
THE VOID

In the eyes of its originators the October Revolution had neither meaning nor future independent of its international function as a catalyst and detonator: it was to be the first spark that would lead to the establishment of socialist regimes in countries which, unlike Russia, possessed an adequate economic infrastructure and cultural basis. Unless it fulfilled this function, the Soviet regime should not even have survived. Lenin often affirmed this belief, and he persisted in this interpretation even after several years had elapsed without bringing any confirmation of his hopes. In June 1921 he

declared that the Socialist Republic might survive amid
capitalist encirclement, "but not for very long, of course." In
February 1922, he was just as categorical as ever: "We have
always proclaimed and repeated this elementary truth of
Marxism, that the victory of socialism requires the joint
efforts of workers in a number of advanced countries."[1]

Russia set out alone on the path of revolution and was
fairly isolated from the beginning, but two factors prevented
a true recognition of the situation: first, the internationalist
notions of the leaders, and second, the persistence for some
time of social agitation in Europe. Even during the civil war,
when Russia, in order to survive, was forced to confront a
kind of capitalist international, the Soviet leaders had not
been aware of their country's isolation. It was only towards
the end of this war that the illusions of the less intellectual and
less internationalist of them began to be dissipated. In the
end they all had to accept the obvious. In the last public
speech of his career, Lenin declared:

"*We are isolated*—we told ourselves. *You are isolated*—
we are told by almost every capitalist country with which we
have concluded any deals, with which we have undertaken
any engagements, with which we have begun any negotia-
tions. And that is where the special difficulty lies. We must
realize this difficulty."[2]

But the fact of this isolation, with its incalculable long-
term consequences, was also to cause certain unforeseen
circumstances and a revision of certain principles. According to the most widespread interpretation of Marxist theory,
the dictatorship of the proletariat, the method of government

[1] V. I. Lenin, *Sochineniya* (Works), 5th ed. (Moscow, Institute of
Marxism-Leninism, 1958–65), Vol. XLIV, pp. 9 and 418. Hereafter
abbreviated as *Soch.*
[2] Speech of November 20, 1922, *Soch.*, Vol. XLV, p. 304.

of the first successful revolution, should be established in a country where the working class formed the majority of the population: the dictatorship of the working class would then be exercised over a negligible minority. Nothing of the kind was possible in Russia, but in fact the Bolsheviks were less embarrassed at admitting this than were the Mensheviks. The Bolsheviks accepted an interpretation of Marx admitting for the backward Germany of the 1850s a possible success for socialism based on "a proletarian revolution flanked by a peasant war." There was even less reason to be anxious about the Russian infrastructure insofar as the revolution, which was easier to launch in such conditions, would soon spread to other countries and would hand over the direction of the movement to fraternal parties that were more worthy of it.

But although the second proposition proved to be false, the first appeared as a result in a new light. The workers undoubtedly played a major role in the seizure of power by the Bolsheviks. Throughout the civil war they continued to provide the Soviet army and administration with their most dedicated cadres. But this war caused an incalculable loss of lives and installations. Many factories were destroyed and production had come to a standstill. The workers, who had led the struggle in every sphere of activity, suffered particularly heavy losses and many of the survivors had dispersed and taken refuge in the countryside. At the same time the most dedicated and most gifted among them had been mobilized by the governmental services, both local and central. The administrative machine considerably reduced the ranks of the working class, especially in the sectors where it recruited its best cadres, the metalworkers, railroad workers and miners. The use of workers in the administrative machine was perhaps the heaviest burden borne by the Russian proletariat, which comprised no more than three million indus-

trial workers. Lenin himself said that the strength of the
proletariat had been sapped above all by the creation of the
state machine,[3] and added that the proletariat had become
déclassé, that is, it had gone off the rails as a class. Whether
the workers had been skilled in combat, absorbed by the
administrative machine or demoralized by shortages and
black-market activities undertaken in order to survive,[4] the
result was tragic in each case. The Revolution, represented
as a seizure of power by the proletariat, which in fact it very
largely was, presented a very different picture at the end of a
civil war as a result of which most of its pioneers had been
killed off. Two years after October, the Soviet had lost the
direct exercise of power. In March 1919, Lenin noted with
deep regret, but with the greatest frankness, that because of
the deplorable level of education among the masses, "the
Soviets, which according to their program were organs of
government *by the workers,* are in fact only organs of government *for the workers* by the most advanced section of the
proletariat, but not by the working masses themselves."[5]

As soon as the fact of the extinction of the proletariat was
admitted, the dictatorship inevitably lost one by one the characteristics that had been attributed to it. In the exercise of
power the dictatorship could only count "on a narrow stratum
of advanced workers," and it would not be able to maintain
itself long on this basis; the Party, in which the workers
formed no more than a large minority, was substituted for the
proletariat; it became both the arm and the sword of the
revolutionary state. "The bourgeoisie," said Lenin, "is well
aware that in fact 'the forces of the working class' consist at
present of the powerful advance guard of this class: the

---

[3] *Soch.,* Vol. XLIV, p. 106.
[4] *Ibid.,* pp. 103 and 106, and Vol. XLIII, p. 310.
[5] *Soch.,* Vol. XXXVIII, p. 170.

Russian Communist Party."[6] On another occasion he wrote that the Party was the strongest root of the dictatorship—which is nothing less than an aberration from the point of view of Marxist theory. Well organized, well led and well disciplined, the local cells and echelons provided both leaders and executants for the struggles waged on every front, for every administrative and economic task. An American historian who is hardly a Communist sympathizer writes: "[The Whites] . . . had to fight an enemy which, despite some difficulties with defection, corruption, and disobedience of orders, still had a corps of trained and disciplined men all over the country in the form of the Communist Party."[7] This was praise indeed for the powerful instrument that Lenin had forged and which now perhaps was developing in a way he had not foreseen. The Party held the real power and was responsible for the exercise of that power. In fact, it became perfectly obvious during the first months of the Revolution, and even before the destruction wrought by the civil war, that the working class alone was not capable of governing, or even of running the factories in which they worked. The works committees, the workers' councils and workers' control—created spontaneously and authentically in the revolutionary enthusiasm that immediately followed the seizure of power as the result of a libertarian upsurge of anarcho-syndicalist inspiration—had been fully legitimized by Lenin in his *State and Revolution*, but they were characterized by a degree of confusion and inefficiency capable of paralyzing the country's productive machinery. It was necessary to abandon this method and adopt another; many saw in this a betrayal of socialist ideals, but Lenin defended his demands

[6] *Ibid.*, Vol. XXXIX, p. 412, and Vol. XLIV, p. 107.
[7] Donald W. Treadgold, *Twentieth Century Russia* (Chicago, Rand McNally & Co., 1959), p. 181.

with the utmost energy—demands for discipline that would
be guaranteed by the rule of the managers (*edinonachalie*)
and the preponderance of administrations. Even before the
mass slaughter of workers in the civil war, a wide breach had
already opened between the theory and practice of the dictatorship of the proletariat. But others were to follow.

We have seen that in one of the foregoing quotations
Lenin wrote the words "the forces of the working class" in
inverted commas. The Party vanguard no longer had the
support of the mass of its troops; its social basis was now in
inverted commas. The more lucid minds in the Party were
well aware that they were in some sense suspended in the
void, but it was one more illusion of the theoreticians to believe that this situation could last for very long. The social
void was soon to be filled by forces other than those originally foreseen.

The industrial managements began to make their presence
felt—though industry was still very weak—but in addition,
there grew up in the local and central government services an
enormous body of functionaries who, according to Lenin,
were former Tsarist bureaucrats, and they were to occupy
an increasingly important place in the political life of the
country. The regime could certainly not do without such an
administrative machine, but, again according to Lenin, it
was not Soviet; it was a shameful anomaly. These Tsarist
functionaries—the Russian term, *chinovniki,* is particularly
expressive of their character—had at first boycotted the new
regime, but later they decided to cooperate with it. "They
came back and our mishaps began there,"[8] said Lenin. We do
not know what would have happened if they had not come
back, but this is what did happen: "At the summit of the

8 *Soch.,* Vol. XLV, p. 290.

power structure we have, we do not know exactly how many, but at least a few thousand, and at the most a few tens of thousands, of our own people. But at the base of the hierarchy, hundreds of thousands of former functionaries that we have inherited from the Tsar and bourgeois society are working, partly consciously, partly unconsciously, against us."[9] Confronted with this network, which had hardly been affected at all by the Soviet influence, Lenin was perplexed and disarmed. Moreover, his analysis is not entirely correct, since this machine became, against the will of the functionaries themselves, a real social support of the state; it carried out more or less efficiently the tasks assigned to it by the state and, in spite of everything, it was linked to the state by the fact that it contained at least some elements that were loyal to the new regime. Another valuable opinion on this subject is provided by Trotsky:

"The demobilization of the Red Army of five million played no small role in the formation of the bureaucracy. The victorious commanders assumed leading posts in the local Soviets, in economy, in education, and they persistently introduced everywhere that regime which had ensured success in the civil war. Thus on all sides the masses were pushed away gradually from actual participation in the leadership of the country."[10]

The place occupied by these ex-Red Army cadres was considerably greater than the figure mentioned by Lenin of some tens of thousands of Communists at the summit of the administrative hierarchy, for they were intermingled at every level with the mass of *chinovniki*.

In fact, Lenin was deeply concerned and displeased at the

[9] *Ibid.*
[10] Leon Trotsky, *The Revolution Betrayed*, trans. by Max Eastman (Garden City, N.Y., Doubleday, Doran & Company, Inc., 1937), pp. 89–90.

way the administration as a whole exercised its power and carried out its everyday tasks, whatever its composition. He was forever criticizing heroes of the civil war who proved incapable of carrying out peacetime tasks—he was the only political leader to do so with impunity. Even in Moscow, where tens of thousands of the best Communist cadres were concentrated, he discovered and rooted out red tape and inefficiency.[11] The Communists were allowing themselves to be smothered by a mass of strangers and were not in effective control of affairs.

"What then is lacking? It is all too clear what the Communist leaders lack: it is culture. Let us take the case of Moscow: 4,700 Communist leaders and an enormous mass of bureaucrats. Who is leading and who is being led? I very much doubt if it can be said that the Communists are leading. I think it can be said that they are being led."[12]

All these phenomena had a profound influence on the mechanism of power: in practice, the Party now exercised absolute power and was outside the control of any social force whatsoever. As the working class became weaker, the Party expanded in membership. Many of these new members were of course workers, but there was also a considerable number of peasants and, above all, of intellectuals and functionaries who came from quite different political backgrounds. The ties with the ideology of the founders were relaxed; on occasion they could be abandoned altogether when vulgar careerists, attracted by the privileges of a party in power, joined their ranks. In the space of a few years the political and cultural level of the Party as a whole must have sunk considerably. The overwhelming majority of the members of the Party "are not politically educated enough . . . for

[11] Cf. *O Prodnaloge, Soch.*, Vol. XLIII, p. 234.
[12] *Soch.*, Vol. XLV, p. 95.

us to have an effectively proletarian leadership at so difficult a time, especially if we take into account the enormous numerical predominance of the peasantry in the country, which is rapidly awakening to an independent class consciousness."[13]

In fact, even if there had been a majority of workers in the Party, it would have made little difference. They would have been incapable of stopping its *petit-bourgeois* decline. Lenin knew this,[14] and his worst fears were that the Party might be drowned in the great flood of the all-powerful Russian *petite bourgeoisie*. On the other hand, he was far less aware of a danger that was appearing from a quite different direction.

The Party, which had to govern the workers that had remained outside its organization, adopted the same attitude towards those workers that had joined its ranks—and this domination was even more apparent in the case of members of other social classes that had been admitted. Most of the workers, even those who were working in key industries and who should therefore in theory have been the strongest pillars of the state, were too ignorant to participate effectively in policy decisions or in the exercise of government. This judgment applies of course to the workers as a group, for individually they held the highest posts in the Party. In this respect the Party remained faithful to its principles and drew its cadres from the working class, even to the extent sometimes of exhausting the source of suitable applicants. It was the same internal elite that could assume both the direction of affairs and the education of Party members, whether they were workers or drawn from other social classes.

The dictatorship of the proletariat, which had been transformed by the pressure of circumstances into a dictatorship

---

[13] *Ibid.*, p. 19.
[14] Cf. *ibid.*, pp. 18, 19.

of a socially diverse minority, soon became a dictatorship of
the Party. But at this stage the gradual narrowing of the
central core of power had not come to an end. In March
1922, in a letter to the members of the Central Committee,
Lenin made a further admission. "It must be recognized,"
he said, "that the Party's proletarian policy is determined at
present not by its rank and file, but by the immense and un-
divided authority of the tiny section that might be called the
Party's Old Guard."[15] But the process was not yet completed.
The strange dynamic that drove the state to an ever increasing
concentration of power among an ever smaller number of
individuals continued to operate. It seems at first sight that the
Soviet regime was dogged by misfortune, but it would be
more accurate to see the causes of this development in a combination of particularly difficult circumstances. The civil war
had a more decisive and more lasting effect on this regime
than is generally believed. Having only just established itself
and while still at a stage when it was very uncertain of its
organization and methods, it had to concentrate all effort on
a single objective in order to survive at all. It cannot be emphasized too much that at the period under discussion the
regime was emerging from the civil war and had been shaped
by that war as much as by the doctrines of the Party, or by
the doctrine on the Party, which many historians have seen
as being Lenin's "original sin."

In the face of large, well-equipped "White" armies supported by several Western countries, a strict centralism and
absolutism became imperative. Yet during this period, discussion within the Party did not stop; its only limitations
were those imposed by the requirements of solidarity against
the enemy. The prohibition of factions and of any discussion

[15] *Ibid.,* p. 20.

of fundamental problems came only after the war. The constantly alarming nature of the situation and the extension of the state of emergency required a constant mobilization of the cadres, their transfer from one front to another, or from a military task to an economic one and vice versa. No democratic procedure would have made these solutions possible, but only authoritarian ones: orders, appointments and dismissals made them possible. These methods, which were sanctioned in no way either by theory or by statute, but which had been practiced for three years, became a reality of Party life. The appointment from above of a secretary of a Party organization became a natural and expected event; local organizations that lacked capable officers themselves sometimes appealed to the hierarchy and asked for leaders to be sent to them; already all important non-Party posts in the country were subject to appointment by the Party leadership. With the return of peace, these habits were not lost and the special bureau (Uchraspred) of the Central Committee that distributed the cadres according to the needs of the state continued to function. The procedure was effective but was to arouse a good deal of protest, for it became very easy for the Secretariat of the Central Committee to send a politically awkward individual—opposed perhaps to a particular line or to one of the leaders—from one post to another, or to a less important or more distant one. The protests that arose, with the launching of the NEP, against a procedure regarded as antidemocratic and contrary to the elective principle enshrined in the Party statutes were ineffectual. To put an end to this state of affairs, which gave the Orgburo, the Organization Bureau, considerable power within the Party, it would have been necessary to undertake a thorough reorganization of the system of direction, one of almost revolutionary proportions.[16] But the introduction of the NEP, in the midst of famine and peasant revolt, with the specter of the Kronstadt uprising in the background, was not yet a suitable moment to relax controls. About March–April 1921 the situation seemed to have deteriorated and Lenin, anxious to avoid a paralysis of the Party—the only fully reliable force at his disposal—forbade factions and gave the Central Committee the right to exclude from the Party members accused of factionism. Whether this decision was a hasty reaction to an emergency, a merely temporary measure,[17] or even the result of misjudgment and a lack of percipience, it was to weigh heavily on the future of the Party and the country. It strengthened still further the Politburo, its Secretariat and its Orgburo. Even the position of the Central Committee itself was weakened. Everything tended more and more to pass through the Politburo; senior civil servants and People's Commissars brought before this supreme authority those matters they were too timid to decide for themselves, and Lenin complained bitterly of the fact before the Eleventh Party Congress.

This situation was at least partially masked by the presence of Lenin in the Sovnarkom, as long as he was able to remain at his post, and the Politburo devoted itself more to the working out of the great lines of national policy and to solving problems of principle. Yet Lenin himself discussed in the Politburo a great many day-to-day problems that were really the province of the Sovnarkom, and when he fell seriously

[16] Cf. E. H. Carr, *Socialism in One Country, 1924–1926* (London, Macmillan & Co. Ltd., 1958–59), Vol. II, Chap. 19, especially pp. 201–4 on the system of nominations.

[17] Cf. E. H. Carr, *The Interregnum: 1923–1924* (New York, The Macmillan Company, 1954), appendix. Trotsky, *The Revolution Betrayed*, p. 96: "This forbidding of factions was again regarded as an exceptional measure to be abandoned at the first serious improvement in the situation."

ill, the Politburo became the key institution of the country. The Secretariat, which directed the current administrative and executive work of the Politburo and Central Committee, appeared to be no more than a secondary mechanism, but with the new practices that had crept into the Party, especially during the civil war, it is clear what enormous power could be wielded by its head.

In April 1922 Stalin was appointed General Secretary, or Gensek in the Party jargon. At this time he was also Commissar for the Nationalities and also, for a time, Commissar for the Workers' and Peasants' Inspection, an impressive accumulation of powers and responsibilities that only the wise Preobrazhensky denounced with any vigor. At this stage we are not very far away from the situation that Trotsky, criticizing Lenin's point of view on the organization of the Party, had foreseen in 1903–1904: "The organization of the Party takes the place of the Party itself; the Central Committee takes the place of the organization; and finally the dictator takes the place of the Central Committee. . . ."[18] Trotsky's only error was to regard Lenin's centralism as an "egocentralism": Lenin's views did not conceal a thirst for personal power, and in fact, the Party machine that Lenin and Trotsky helped to build turned against both of them.

Again in order to understand more fully Lenin's political thinking during the last months of his life, we should now turn to another aspect of the phenomenon of the concentration of power. The Bolsheviks sincerely believed in the theory of the dictatorship of the proletariat. The substitution of the Party for the proletariat, at first a sheer matter of fact, had to be introduced, not without a certain ambiguity, into the

[18] Bertram D. Wolfe, *Three Who Made a Revolution* (Boston, Beacon Press, 1955), p. 253.

theory; it was regarded as a temporary phenomenon that
would disappear when the workers were reorganized in the
large factories and when industry was strengthened by its
future achievements. In fact, it initiated managerial rule in
the factories and in the country as a whole, and the bureaucracy began its long reign. Lenin explained this situation by
the lack of adequate economic bases. This proposition was
not too embarrassing while there were prospects of revolution in Europe, but later this handicap was to prove tragic.
Lenin said that although Russia possessed the most advanced
political regime in the world, it had not yet succeeded in
creating even the foundations of a national economy; the
obvious absence of the bases of socialism almost meant that
nothing had been achieved definitively: "The adverse forces
of a moribund capitalism could still regain power from us."[19]
Thus the basic terms of historical materialism were inverted
by its most faithful disciples. The socioeconomic bases indispensable to the realization of the official aims of the state
were cruelly lacking. The new state was suspended in a kind
of "two-storied void," the first being the absence of a proletariat and the second that of an economic infrastructure. As
E. H. Carr has remarked, the dictatorship was *in posse*
rather than *in esse*.[20] This was very far from the optimistic,
utopian and simplified notions expressed in Lenin's *State
and Revolution* in 1917, in which all problems seemed to
have been solved in advance by the example of the Paris
Commune. Militants used to deducing the political from the
economic and social found themselves in a disturbing situation in which a governing elite devoid of any social basis
embodied a kind of "pure political power" and imposed its
will on a society whose spontaneous dynamic, under the

[19] *Soch.*, Vol. XLIV, p. 418.
[20] *Socialism in One Country*, Vol. I, pp. 103–4.

NEP, tended towards ends that were the opposite of those of the Party.

Lenin and Leninist doctrine had to adapt themselves to this new situation. Two things helped them to do this: the importance of the role attributed to political consciousness, which is not spontaneous, and a certain concept of the Party that attributed to it the task of awakening this consciousness. The central place accorded to the Party in the Leninist strategy and the somewhat voluntarist interpretation that Leninism gave Marxism should not, however, lead us to impute to it, as sometimes has been done, all the responsibility for phenomena such as the gradual shrinking of political power that eventually culminated in an autocracy. Leninist doctrine did not originally envisage a monolithic state, nor even a strictly monolithic party; the dictatorship of the Party *over* the proletariat was never part of Lenin's plans, it was the completely unforeseen culmination of a series of unforeseen circumstances. Despite Trotsky's perceptive intuition, it is not true that the concentration of power that reached its apogee with the Stalinist regime was the result of the ideas and splits of 1903–1904. It is in the history of a later period, in the events that followed the Revolution and the way in which they molded theory, that its origin is to be found. Neither the theory of "war communism" nor the diametrically opposite notions on which the NEP was based have any connection with pre-Revolutionary preoccupations and theories. Once peace had been re-established with internal victory, Lenin set about underpinning political power by the acquisition of an economic infrastructure and the raising of the cultural level of the cadres and of the people—beginning with the problem of illiteracy. Lenin knew that in the situation in which his regime found itself, the political preceded the economic, but the idea that such a preponderance could

last indefinitely gave him no reassurance. He was not resigned
to using for very long the lever, political power alone, that
many in our period regard as the most powerful and most
decisive.[21]

On this point a further deception awaited the militants as
they emerged from their illusions concerning "war communism." The need to construct the foundations lacking in
the social edifice precluded the possibility of any direct introduction of socialism, let alone communism. Lenin calmed
the impatient by repeating that it was merely the beginning
of a transitional period, during which he would sanction the
prolongation of the policy of the NEP. And yet he saw very
clearly the terrible dangers in which it placed the regime:
external threats and internal instability (of the peasants in
particular), but also the danger presented by a possible degeneration of the Communists themselves under the pressure
of a corrupting environment. Pursuing his idea that the Communists were no longer the leaders but the led, Lenin declared before the Eleventh Party Congress:

"Something has happened rather like what we learned in
our history lessons when we were children: one people sub-
jugates another. The subjugator is then a conquering people
and the subjugated a vanquished people. This is true enough,
but what happens to the culture of these two peoples? The
answer is not so simple. If the conquering people is more
cultured than the vanquished people, the stronger imposes
its culture on the weaker. But in the opposite case, the vanquished country may impose its culture on the conqueror. Is
this not what happened in the capital of the RSFSR, and were

[21] The primacy of politics over economics in a sense that surely differs
from the classic Marxist notion is clearly expressed by Lenin, notably in
"Our Revolution," *Soch.*, Vol. XLV, pp. 378–82, and in the text reproduced in Appendix IX. Cf. also Carr, *Socialism in One Country*, Vol. I,
pp. 130–31.

not 4,700 of the best Communists (almost a division) submerged by an alien culture? Is it true that one might have the impression that the culture of the vanquished is of a high level? Not so: it is wretched and insignificant. But it is still superior to ours."[22]

This speech shows that Lenin was sharply aware of the dangers that beset his regime. Even if later historical developments were rather different from what he anticipated, it must be recognized that Lenin was a man who analyzed the situation first and then told the Party and the whole country the plain truth of the situation as he saw it.

[22] *Soch.*, Vol. XLV, pp. 95–96.

2
THE NEP:
AN
ENIGMA

In the conditions prevailing at the end of the civil war the Soviet leaders were presented with a number of problems demanding solutions. How were they to avoid a confrontation with the Western powers in the period preceding new revolutions in Europe or Asia? How were they to prevent the degeneration of the state, or rather, how were they to preserve the ideological and moral purity of the party now in power? How could they escape the scourge of bureaucracy? There were no ready solutions to problems that involved so many unknown factors, but things became still more complicated with the introduction of the original and unexpected economic system known as the "New Economic Policy." This policy was adopted in face of the urgent need to remedy the stagnation into which the country as a whole, but agriculture in particular, had fallen. After two years in operation it was to prove salutary, but for the Bolsheviks it was a pact with the devil.

Lenin explained that it was a measure, intended to save the country from disaster, by which the peasants were given the necessary concessions to encourage them to resume production and feed the country; and these concessions could be seen as the injection of a dose of capitalism—"a capitalism that we must and can accept, and to which we can and must assign certain limits, for it is necessary to the great mass of the peasantry and to the trade that enables the peasants' needs to be satisfied. We must arrange things in such a way that the regular operation of the economy and patterns of exchange characteristic of capitalism become possible. It must be so for the sake of the people. Otherwise we should not be able to live. . . . For them, for the peasant camp, nothing else is absolutely necessary; as for the rest, they must make the best of it."[1]

What Lenin was doing was something that has rarely been seen in history. He was allowing the peasants a strong dose of capitalism in exchange for "the rest," that is, in exchange for leaving political power in the hands of the Bolsheviks. It was an advantageous operation certainly, but it was also a dangerous one. Many militants feared that such a remedy, while salutary for the patient, would prove mortal for the doctor. The decision aroused considerable speculation throughout the world; the enemies of the regime were led to

[1] *Soch.*, Vol. XLV, pp. 85–86.

hope that in reintroducing capitalism the NEP would bring about the end of Bolshevism. At first, every section of opinion within the Party accepted this solution as the only possible one, but many soon came to regard it as a betrayal, an alliance contrary to nature. In any case, the Party was worried, and not without reason, for now the illusions created by "war communism" were shattered: the peasant market and private enterprise were to be re-established and the capitalist spirit would not fail to penetrate every sector of Soviet life and act as an element of corruption and dissolution, affecting the state and even the Party. Many would have endorsed the view of Rosa Luxemburg (expressed in 1918): "The Leninist agrarian reform has created a new and powerful layer of popular enemies of socialism on the countryside, enemies whose resistance will be much more dangerous and stubborn than that of the noble large landowners."[2]

It will be seen that Lenin, without questioning the need for the reform, says very much the same thing of the peasants. The Russian peasantry, with little interest in socialist experiments, largely illiterate, and what is more, very unproductive, formed a mass of some hundred million people in which there always smoldered a certain spirit of revolt, a *pugachev-shchina,* that had often troubled the tranquillity of the Tsars. The NEP had the advantage of establishing freedom of commerce, but it seemed to have increased even more the political inconveniences of the land parcellation caused by the reform; it had the effect of making the capitalist economy still more attractive to the peasants and of driving them still further away from the collectivist principles of the Party.

But there was worse to come. The NEP succeeded in regenerating the capitalist class, businessmen, tradesmen, in-

[2] Rosa Luxemburg, *The Russian Revolution* (Ann Arbor, University of Michigan Press, 1961), p. 46.

dustrialists, old and new. Thus the Revolution not only
continued to disappoint the proletariat,[3] but it also provided
the peasantry with an anti-Bolshevist rallying point and the
necessary leaders for a revolt in the event of any conflict
with the state being settled to their disadvantage. No one had
forgotten the danger of seeing the peasantry siding with the
nepmany, or new bourgeoisie, and the traditional bourgeois
cadres who were still hostile to the regime, aided perhaps by
the capitalist countries, which still benefitted from an overwhelming economic and military superiority. The NEP was
like a mine that had been placed under the still insecure
structure of the new regime.[4] Whether he would have admitted it or refuted it in public, Lenin was no less concerned
than other militants at the prospect of such a threat. The
NEP was a bet that was not won in advance. People continued to ask themselves, with Lenin, the question *"Kto
kogo?"*—"Who will win?"—but this time on the home front.

Meanwhile, in the hope of reaching at last a period of
peaceful construction, the Bolsheviks made a considerable
effort. During the period from March 1921, when the NEP
was introduced, to the appearance of the first glimmers of
hope with the good harvest of 1922 and a certain appease-
ment of the peasantry, a strenuous attempt was made to ex-
plore new methods of administration and to find remedies for
past failures. But it was also a period of great theoretical
confusion among the militants. A good many ideas and doctrines previously held had been exploded under pressure
from the facts. It was necessary to re-examine the major
question concerning the very character of the October Revo-

[3] Lenin confirmed publicly in 1921 that so far it was the peasants, and
not the workers—who had the heaviest burden to bear—that had most
profited from the Revolution. Cf. *Soch.,* Vol. XLIV, p. 46. This was to
prove even more true the following year.

[4] Cf. Chapter I, note 20.

lution. Lenin did not escape the confusion; he recognized it while being its victim. In August 1921, he wrote that the Revolution had been bourgeois-democratic between November 1917 and January 5, 1918 (Constituent Assembly); the socialist stage had then begun with the establishment of proletarian democracy. But another chronology similar to that adopted in autumn 1918 is suggested in the same article: the socialist stage was reached when the movement of the Committees of the Poor, or Kombedy, had won the class struggle against the kulaks in the countryside. But it should not be forgotten that the Kombedy were abolished at the end of 1918.[5] Two months after this article was written, in October 1921, yet another chronology appears. This time, the bourgeois-democratic stage of the Revolution is seen as having been completed only in 1921. And a little later, we find a slightly different version: the October Revolution was fully a proletarian revolution, but it accomplished the tasks of a bourgeois-democratic revolution *"en passant."*[6] There is really nothing very surprising about such uncertainties; only the long-term results of the October Revolution could enable its true character to be determined. Another point: how could the NEP be justified from a theoretical point of view; what strategic definition could be given it? Was it a "retreat" in relation to the preceding period—in which case the Party was abandoning neither the aims nor the methods of "war communism," which at the most were regarded as premature? Or, on the contrary, had the Party returned to the more correct line adopted in the spring of 1918—in which case "war communism" was merely a policy of expediency that

[5] The article of August 1921 is reproduced in *Soch.*, Vol. XLIV, pp. 101–2. On November 6, 1918, Lenin declared to the Congress of Soviets: "The October revolution of the towns became a true October revolution for the countryside only in autumn 1918." *Soch.*, Vol. XXXVII, p. 144.

[6] *Soch.*, Vol. XLIV, pp. 102, 145, 147.

had proved largely erroneous?[7] Lenin did not opt very clearly for either of these two ideas, but in his last speech he came back to the "retreat" theory.[8]

All this does not provide an adequate explanation of the NEP. Surely in this long period of transition an initial strategic retreat was necessary so as to prepare for a further advance. Lenin tried to put a little order in all this confusion by advancing the theory of "state capitalism," which he formulated in his pamphlet *On Taxation in Kind,* published at the time of the launching of NEP. This did not mean, however, that the "beginning of the socialist stage" theory was abandoned. The theory of "state capitalism," already used after the February Revolution and again at the beginning of 1918, was inspired by the experience of the extensively and strictly state-controlled German war economy. In the context of the Soviet economy, however, there was a substantial difference: the state was not a capitalist but a proletarian one and directly occupied important economic positions.

Lenin used the term "state capitalism" because he was counting on the cooperation of Russian capitalism and, even more so, of large foreign capitalist interests; he thought that Russia needed a long period of capitalist development in order to assimilate organizational methods and technical expertise, and to acquire the capital and the intellectual abilities that the Workers' State did not yet possess. Obviously, the state must remain constantly vigilant and create the necessary methods of supervision and control. Thus Lenin hoped to build socialism with the help of "foreign hands," who, he thought, would not reject his offers if it was

[7] Cf. E. H. Carr, *The Bolshevik Revolution: 1917–1923* (New York, The Macmillan Company, 1952), Vol. II, pp. 273–78.
[8] *Soch.,* Vol. XLV, p. 302.

made worth their while to accept them. Another peculiarity of this theory helped to make its reception by certain of the other leaders, including Preobrazhensky, Bukharin and Trotsky, somewhat critical or reserved. According to Lenin, the principal enemy of the state was no longer big capital but the unruly, fragmented *petit bourgeois* sector that eluded all state planning and control. Only big capital possessed the qualities that were useful to progress: its ability to organize on a large scale, its tendency to plan and its sense of discipline. This was why the Workers' State should conclude an alliance with it in order to combat the pernicious influence of the already tottering *petite bourgeoisie*. Lenin said: "The proletarian state must form a bloc or an alliance with 'state capitalism' against the *petit bourgeois* element." And earlier in the same year, he quoted an opinion already expressed in 1918, that "in our country the main enemy of socialism is the *petit bourgeois* element."[9]

It is important to realize, of course, that the *petite bourgeoisie* referred to is none other than the peasantry. What had become, then, of the strategic necessity, which was also regarded as fundamental and constantly reiterated in the slogans, of an alliance with the peasantry? In the course of history, Stalin was to resolve this profound contradiction by the methods which suited him best. Lenin proposed others, but he was unable to apply them himself.

In the immediate future the ambiguous theory of state capitalism was to undergo a curious fate. It had been conceived to fulfill several functions at once: first, to dissipate any illusion as to the so-called socialist character of Soviet society, and secondly, to formulate in Marxist terms the nature of the transitional period Russia was then going

---

[9] *Soch.*, Vol. XLIV, p. 108, and Vol. XLIII, p. 206.

through and to define how this period would lead Russia to
socialism, the conditions for which had not yet been created.
The notion of state capitalism as the most advanced political
and social form of capitalism, and by that very fact, the stage
that directly preceded socialism, could fulfill these functions
of clarification and explanation provided that the theory
was verified in the specific conditions of Russia. But two years
later, contradicted by the facts, it had to be abandoned.
Having failed to obtain the cooperation of big capital, Lenin
set out to win the cooperation of the peasantry. We shall
return to this question later; let us be content for the moment
to remark that the NEP proved beneficial for the economic
life of the country; a period of peaceful construction seemed
to have begun without anyone knowing exactly how long it
could last. Without expressing himself very strongly on the
matter, Lenin seemed to admit that in the conditions of
capitalist encirclement it would "obviously not be for very
long."[10]

To succeed in this undertaking it was necessary to reorganize, above all in a practical way. In such a totally new
situation, experience, the structures of reference and the
whole scientific basis necessary for the drawing up of pro-
grams of action were lacking. The first evil to cure—and the
most frequently denounced—was that of bureaucracy. Lenin
admitted, "We do not know how to do this."[11] For a time he
believed that the initiative would come from the provinces.
It seemed to him that it was easier to experience and learn
good management methods in administratively smaller units,
for "the evil of bureaucracy concentrates naturally at the
center." But confronted with the facts, Lenin soon changed

[10] *Ibid.*, Vol. XLIV, p. 9. Cf. Chapter I, note I, and pages 3–4. In
other passages, however, he shows himself to be more optimistic.
[11] *Soch.*, Vol. XLIII, p. 234.

his view, and without ceasing to denounce Moscow as the
capital of baneful bureaucratic red tape, he strongly criticized obscurantist and corrupting local influences and the
way in which they settled their accounts.[12] It was necessary,
therefore, to fall back on the more advanced workers, on the
proletarian elite, or rather on the Party. With the support
that it enjoyed of a section of the workers and poor peasants
—and taking advantage of the neutrality of the mass of the
peasantry obtained through the NEP—a new start could be
made on new bases. The elite was to be provided with clear
theoretical ideas and wide government responsibilities. If
necessary, it must use terror in order to "organize coercion
in the interest of the workers,"[13] according to an old formula
dating from 1917.

For the moment the first weapon of the elite, namely, a
clear program of action, did not exist. In his last public
appearance Lenin asked the question, "How can we reorganize?" and he answered, "We do not yet know." The other
weapon, to which one could always have recourse, was also
to be adapted to a period of peaceful construction and market
economy. Lenin began to reorganize the Cheka and to reduce
its powers. The biggest problem was still to be solved: how
to preserve the purity of an elite that possessed absolute
power. Where could guarantees be found against its possible
degeneration?

[12] *Soch.,* Vol. XLV, p. 199.
[13] A formula used on November 21, 1917. *Soch.,* Vol. XXXV, p. 110.

3

THE
ECLIPSE
OF
LENIN

The formidable administrative machine created from scratch in the course of the civil war was a decisive factor in the Bolshevik victory. However often and however strongly Lenin criticized it, he was obliged to admit that it was in itself a success. He declared that the victory achieved during the years 1917–1921 would have been impossible without the creation of the state war machine. He even added that "it was a great and exalting work."[1] But in the Russia of those days history was quickly made and one crisis followed an-

[1] *Soch.*, Vol. XLIV, p. 106.

other; a favorable factor soon became a curse and brought
with it bitter fruit. The consequences of the war also fell upon
the personnel of the Party leadership. Before long it was clear
that leaders of a particular type were emerging as dominant
among the men who rose in the hierarchy. They had to know
how to be harsh, they had to be good organizers, and they
had to show that they were capable of using, without being
too scrupulous, the enormous powers that a wartime dictatorship conferred on them, since what was wanted of them
was the ability to win at all costs and not to reason or hesitate.

The end of the war did not make itself felt at once as a
relaxation. The consciousness that a new period had just
begun appeared only during the next two years. The establishment of the NEP was presented as an emergency measure
taken to avoid catastrophe. It was quite natural, therefore,
that for some time the government machine should continue
to function as before. The fact that the prohibition of factions
was made only after the civil war shows only too clearly that
the prevailing psychology was one of a struggle for existence.
A number of men were dropped from, or left, the Secretariat
and Central Committee. Among them were the three secretaries of the Central Committee, Krestinsky, Preobrazhensky
and Serebryakov—all three future members of the Left
Opposition and future victims of the Stalinist purges. And
significantly, Kaganovich, Uglanov, Yaroslavsky and Molotov rose to the highest positions. They were all future Stalinists; they all belonged to the "race" of realistic and practical
men of action.[2]

Aside from the Party, the civil war had left the country
with only one more or less adequate defense: the state admin-

---

[2] Uglanov, however, after helping Stalin most effectively to defeat the
Left Opposition, became a Bukharinite in 1928.

istrative machine. Everything else had to be reconstructed and reconsidered. But the administrative machine and, now more than before, the Party machine were moving in the direction of increasing dictatorial rigidity. At first, no doubt, this process conformed to Lenin's wishes; but more and more, tendencies were appearing, sometimes without his knowledge and sometimes against his will, against which he was ill-equipped to fight; for after three appalling years of war, struggle, work and anxiety, he fell ill.

He fell seriously ill towards the end of 1921 and was forced to rest for several weeks. During the first half of the following year, his capacity for work was reduced and was constantly deteriorating. Then suddenly, on May 25, 1922, catastrophe struck: his right hand and leg became paralyzed and his speech was impaired, sometimes completely so. His convalescence was slow and tedious. "You understand," Lenin later remarked to Trotsky, "I could not even speak or write, and I had to learn everything all over again."[3] His robust constitution saved him once more, but he did not return to work until October 2 and he never fully regained his health. The symptoms of fatigue and discomfort that he showed, his frequent absences from meetings, and the gravity of his last attack did not pass unnoticed by the members of the Sovnarkom and Politburo. The problem of the succession was now no doubt openly discussed among the small circle of leaders. Lenin's first public reappearance was a great effort for him. Alfred Rosmer, who saw him on the platform at the Fourth Congress of the International on November 13, 1922, says this:

"Those who were seeing him for the first time said, 'This is still the same Lenin!' But for the others no such illusion was

[3] Trotsky, *My Life* (New York, Charles Scribner's Sons, 1930), p. 475.

possible; instead of the alert Lenin they had known, the man before them now was strongly affected by paralysis, his features remained immobile, and his general appearance was that of an automaton; his usual simple, rapid, confident speech was replaced by a hesitant, jerky delivery. The comrade who had been given the task of assisting him did so badly; Radek pushed him away and took his place himself."[4]

The return to public life was not to last for long. On December 13, Lenin again fell ill and this time was forced to retire definitively. It is clear therefore that his participation in affairs during 1922 was very limited. It is an important fact to remember in any attempt to understand a period that played so crucial a role in the history of the Soviet Union. The government machine created under Lenin, much more as a product of circumstances than of premeditated decision, continued to operate without his participation. His comrades in the Politburo became used to making their own decisions and acquired a taste for this independence that had been brought about by the absence of the "old man." But their manner, their style of action, continued to be based on previous experience and practice.

At the beginning of 1922, Lenin accepted and perhaps even himself suggested the nomination of Stalin to the post of General Secretary. This post was not yet as important as it was later to become, but it increased considerably in importance in the course of the year, perhaps to the surprise of Lenin himself, whose absence was largely responsible for it. As Lenin was losing his capacity for work and the conduct of affairs was slipping increasingly from his hands, Stalin was gaining in ease and assurance, often in opposition to Lenin.

[4] Alfred Rosmer, *Moscou sous Lénine* (Paris, Pierre Horay, 1953), p. 231.

He was surrounding himself with men of his own choice—a kind of cabal that had already come into being during the civil war. Some of the members of the Politburo were not even aware of this. But it becomes very apparent when one examines the so-called "foreign trade" affair and even more the tangled Georgian conflict. On both occasions Lenin had to fight against his colleagues to defend his positions, and they both reflect the problems of the regime at the time of the eclipse of its supreme head.

The problem of the monopoly of foreign trade became particularly acute towards the end of 1921, when Milyutin, the Soviet delegate at the Riga talks, promised that this monopoly would be abolished.[5] It is not known who gave him instructions to do so, but it is likely that a majority of the Party leaders wanted to settle this question in the general spirit of the NEP. Bukharin, Sokolnikov, Frumkin and others, doubting the capacity of the Commissariat of Foreign Trade to handle international economic exchanges successfully and anxious that such exchanges should be entered upon as soon as possible, advocated either the relaxation of the monopoly or its complete abolition. Stalin too was in favor of one of these theses. But Lenin saw this as a major error, an inadmissible infringement of the country's interests. In his opinion, it was not only unwise but probably harmful to allow foreign exporters to enter into direct contact with private businessmen inside the country, the *nepmany,* for then "the foreigners will buy up and take home with them everything of any value." But the most striking argument concerned the real social basis in Russia, namely the peasantry. Smugglers would no doubt break the trade monopoly in any case—those

[5] *Soch.,* Vol. XLIV, pp. 562–63.

supporting its relaxation insisted on this point—but, again according to Lenin, they consisted of no more than a handful of specialists, and it would be quite a different matter "to have to deal with the entire peasantry that will defend itself as one man and fight against the state that tries to deprive it of its own interest."[6]

Lenin added proof upon proof in an attempt to persuade the Central Committee of the correctness of his views. Only the strict maintenance of the monopoly would remedy the economic weakness of the country. One had to consider the ability of foreigners to offer special prices, not to mention conditions in the international market that were in themselves very advantageous for the Russian agricultural producer. The slightest breach in the defenses would end by destroying the already weak national industries, and help to forge an alliance between the forces of international capitalism and the Russian businessmen on the one hand and the mass of the Russian peasantry on the other against the power of the Soviets.

In March, Lenin's arguments seemed to have carried the day and the monopoly was confirmed by a series of decrees; but in fact it was nothing more than a truce. Lenin realized with some concern that government circles and the Central Committee continued to discuss the matter and to question the solution decided on by constantly formulating new projects for legislative changes. These incessant equivocations considerably damaged the standing of the Soviet trade delegates in their talks with foreign businessmen. Krestinsky, then the representative in Berlin, informed Lenin of this. Foreigners, supposing that the foreign trade monopoly was

[6] Secret letter to Kamenev, March 3, 1922, published for the first time in 1959 (*Soch.*, Vol. XLIV, p. 427). See also the letter addressed to Stalin on October 13, 1922, published in 1950 (*Soch.*, Vol. XLV, p. 221).

about to be abolished, probably preferred to wait until they could make direct contact with private businessmen rather than deal with the Soviet government, which in this field was something of an unknown quantity. Lenin was most annoyed and wrote to Stalin demanding that the monopoly principle be reaffirmed and that all projects of a contrary nature be dropped at once.[7] It was perhaps on this occasion that Lenin discovered that the Gensek was not at all in agreement with him and was asserting his own point of view with increasing assurance. To Lenin's letter Stalin added the following remarks: "At this stage I am not opposed to the strict prohibition of measures that would lead to the weakening of the monopoly of foreign trade. I think however that such a weakening is becoming inevitable."[8] Lenin's theses were adopted by the Politburo on May 22, but during his long absence after his first attack of paralysis, the opponents of the monopoly finally won the day. A few days after Lenin's return to work, at a meeting of the Central Committee on October 6, Sokolnikov's theses proposing considerable reductions in the state trade monopoly were ratified by the plenum. Lenin was ill and absent from the meeting. He felt this decision as a personal blow. As usual, he threw himself into the battle to reverse the Central Committee's decision and began to prepare the ground for the next plenary session.

First he had to get the Central Committee's approval for the question to reappear on its next agenda. To achieve his ends, Lenin sent letter after letter to the members of the Politburo, to the *tsekisty* (the members of the Central Committee), and to senior civil servants; he met with Stalin and other leaders; he canvassed support, often in a very discreet

[7] Letter to Stalin, May 15, 1922, unknown until 1959 (*Soch.*, Vol. XLV, p. 188).
[8] *Ibid.*, p. 548.

way, among the more important members of the government. After his return to work, these activities took up most of his time. Significantly, on October 11, he asked Trotsky to come and confer with him—on this problem in particular. Two days later, he sent an urgent letter to the Politburo demanding in categorical terms the reversal of the decision. The bureau was forced to give ground: it decided to put Lenin's request to a vote of the Central Committee. Once again, Stalin appended a note to Lenin's letter: "Comrade Lenin's letter has not made me change my mind as to the correctness of the decision of the plenum . . . concerning external trade."[9] In the end, however, he gave in, as did most of the *tsekisty,* and agreed to allow the question to be re-examined, "in view of Comrade Lenin's insistence on a revision." So the majority of the Central Committee acceded to Lenin's "earnest request," which enabled him, before the next meeting, to organize his supporters and to "work" on the members of the Central Committee; but his health was worsening and he knew that he would be unable to attend the plenum. Knowing that Trotsky was also a defender of the monopoly, he suggested on December 12 that they should join forces. Trotsky agreed at once, but seized the opportunity to bring up his old idea that the role of the Gosplan should be strengthened particularly in the regulation of foreign trade. Lenin preferred to put off this second question, contenting himself with hinting that he was ready to make concessions. Having established an agreement on principle, Lenin insisted, in increasingly cordial terms, that Trotsky should take on the task of defending their theses, whatever their divergences on the subject of the Gosplan might be: "At any rate, I earnestly

[9] Quoted by Fotieva, *Iz Vospominaniy o Lenine* (Moscow, Goz Izd. Polit. Lit., 1964), pp. 28–29. The letter is reproduced here in Appendix IV.

ask you to take upon yourself, at the coming plenum, the defense of our common opinion."[10] Between December 12 and 15 the two men corresponded with each other at great length, as well as with a number of senior civil servants who had come round to Lenin's thesis. (Meanwhile, it must be remembered, Lenin was making plans to retire from his governmental duties.) If the attempt failed, it was agreed that they would present their case to the Communist caucus at the next Congress of Soviets and later to the Party Congress.

On December 15 Lenin concluded: "Comrade Trotsky, I think we have arrived at a full agreement. I ask you to announce our solidarity in the plenum." In a postscript, he added that he strongly rejected any attempt to equivocate and to adjourn the debate once more, under the pretext of his illness and the importance of waiting until he could take part himself in the discussion. "I should be ten thousand times more upset by a delay which would make completely unstable our policy upon one of the fundamental questions."[11] The same day, in a letter to Stalin and other members of the Central Committee, he announced that he had taken the necessary steps to retire, but—and it must have caused a sensation among the *tsekisty*—he declared: "I have also come to an agreement with Trotsky on the defense of my views on the monopoly of foreign trade."[12]

---

[10] The first letter from Lenin to Trotsky concerning the monopoly was written on December 12. Trotsky replied the same day. The following day, Lenin wrote to him again, confirming their agreement on the subject of the monopoly but expressing his reticence on the problem of the Gosplan. These letters were published by Trotsky in *The Stalin School of Falsification* (New York, Pioneer Publishers, 1937), pp. 58–63. They also appear in *Soch.*, Vols. XLV and LIV, with the exception of one letter that appears in Trotsky.

[11] *Soch.*, Vol. LIV, pp. 325–26.

[12] *Soch.*, Vol. XLV, p. 338.

In the Central Committee and in the Politburo, the problem of the succession secretly preoccupied the leaders. Trotsky, who, thanks to Lenin, was scoring points, merely succeeded in arousing even greater hostility among Lenin's former companions in exile and the old clandestine militants. The "Old Bolsheviks," in whose eyes Trotsky was merely an arrogant, unbearable intruder, closed their ranks after Lenin's letter. The shape of the future triumvirate of Stalin, Kamenev and Zinoviev, based only on hatred of Trotsky and a determination to bar him from power, began to appear during these days.[13] In fact Lenin had gone even further in another postscript to his letter, reaffirming his hostility to any adjournment of the discussion, assured as he was, he said, that "Trotsky will uphold my views as well as I."[14] Such statements could not fail to increase tension and to spread mistrust and jealousy in the Politburo.

On December 18, the Central Committee, in a plenary session, annulled its previous decision, which had caused Lenin so much anxiety. Stalin had given in all along the line. This was already his usual tactic when he felt himself in an inferior position. Lenin, now bedridden, but delighted with his success, congratulated Trotsky warmly: "It seems we captured the position without firing a shot by mere movements of maneuver. I propose that we should not stop but continue the attack."[15] The consequences of this letter, which caused Stalin to lose his nerve, will become apparent later.

---

[13] This is not the place for a study of the relations between Trotsky and the other members of the Politburo during Lenin's illness. This matter is fully dealt with in the relevant chapters in Isaac Deutscher, *The Prophet Unarmed: Trotsky, 1921–1929* (New York: Oxford University Press, 1959); Carr, *Interregnum,* and Robert V. Daniels, *The Conscience of the Revolution* (Cambridge, Mass., Harvard University Press, 1960).

[14] *Soch.,* Vol. XLIV, p. 339.

[15] *Soch.,* Vol. LIV, pp. 327–28.

For the moment we must be content to draw a few conclusions from this "battle of the monopoly."

In the first place, it can be said that although Lenin envisaged a long period of application for the NEP, he was aware nonetheless of the dangers that it presented to the regime. The alliance with the peasantry could not be achieved without making concessions to it, but on the other hand concessions could not be made without maintaining certain other safety precautions. There must therefore be no freedom in foreign trade. Such freedom would deprive the state of any means of controlling either prices or the peasant producer. There was no need either for the peasants to enjoy political freedom: "Without capitalism, the peasantry can neither live nor produce, but it can do so, we believe, without hearing the propaganda of the Social Revolutionaries and Mensheviks." In this sphere Lenin had no wish either to lure anyone or to practice demagogy: "We promise neither freedom nor democracy."[16] Notice that this denial is clearly intended as provisional, applicable only so long as the threat of war persists and the regime is not entirely secure from attack.[17]

The second point that a study of the foreign trade affair has helped to elucidate concerns the nature of Lenin's leadership. It has been seen that Lenin's opinions and proposals were not adopted automatically; he was often obliged to defend them against other members of the leadership, which at this period was still genuinely collective, despite Lenin's own pre-eminent position: the other members of the Politburo especially, but also other *tsekisty,* were free to state their opinions and to try and get them passed by a majority. Lenin, like the others, had to look for support, maneuver and per-

[16] *Soch.,* Vol. XLV, p. 120.
[17] See *ibid.,* pp. 53–54.

suade for his proposals to be accepted, before he could be assured of their ultimate success. Because of his immense prestige, his skill as a tactician and his gifts of persuasion, it is true that he usually prevailed in most of the cases in which a problem of principle was at stake. When necessary, Lenin even went so far as to organize the supporters of his theses in a way that could have been regarded as factionalist if anyone had dared to make such an accusation against him. The methods used, however, would have seemed perfectly normal had it not been for the prohibition of factions. It is often said that Lenin was "master of Russia." We should add that he was not a dictator in his party, but its leader. His leadership was incontestable and uncontested but it demanded of him a constant effort of thought and organization; he had to act as if he was reaffirming and reconquering it each day.

A year of illness did not of course diminish his prestige, but it weakened his real grip on affairs. Opposing Lenin became a means of affirming oneself—and Stalin made good use of it during the year in question. In fact, he used it a good deal more often than was realized before the publication of recent Soviet papers. When Lenin found himself in a minority on a question that he thought was of fundamental importance, he sought the aid of Trotsky against Stalin and other leaders; it was to Trotsky that he turned when he was in distress. The second conflict that we are about to examine illustrates these phenomena even more clearly.

4

STALIN,
TROTSKY
AND THE
GEORGIANS

During the years 1920–1921, the relations between the six national Republics—the Ukraine, Byelorussia, Georgia, Azerbaijan, Armenia and the Russian Federation (the RSFSR)—were not defined very clearly, but were regulated by a series of bilateral treaties between the Russian Federation and each of the other five republics. By means of these treaties cooperation was established in the fields of the economy, defense and foreign policy. The government of each republic had a structure that paralleled that of the Russian government. The central direction of the state was assured in practice by the Central Committees of the Parties of each republic, which directed the local governments, but were subject to the Central Committee and Politburo in Moscow by ties of internal Party discipline. The second factor making for the cohesion and security of the regime was the centralization of the army, though implicitly the Republics were authorized to possess separate military units.

The three Caucasian republics, with which we are particularly concerned here, did not become Soviet until 1920—and in the case of Georgia not until the beginning of 1921—when they were conquered by the Red Army, with the fairly general complicity of the local Communists and of the Russian working-class population that predominated in the industrial centers of these countries. Ordzhonikidze had been both the political and the military leader on the Caucasian front during the civil war. It was he who had directed the military conquest of the Caucasian republics for the Soviet regime. After the war he stayed there and represented Moscow in the region as head of the Caucasian bureau of the Party, the Kavburo. In 1921, on grounds of increased efficiency, Lenin urged the Kavburo to proceed to the economic unification of the three republics, especially in the fields of communications, postal services and foreign trade, into a Transcaucasian Federation; the regional leadership of the Party would be renamed the Zakkraykom. Ordzhonikidze applied himself enthusiastically to this task, using all the experience he had acquired and some of the methods he had learned during the civil war and its aftermath. But although a Georgian himself, he came up against opposition from the Georgian Party Central Committee, which, while approving of ties with Russia and the Soviet system, was concerned that attributes of national independence should be preserved.

The Georgian Communists were anxious to gain popular support in a Caucasus in which national and nationalistic feelings were particularly deep-rooted and had recently been reawakened by the experience of independence under a Menshevik government that had just been crushed by force. Accordingly, they affirmed more strongly than any other national group in the Party the principle of independence within the framework of the Soviet system. Moreover, the opposition of the Georgians to Ordzhonikidze was particularly exacerbated by the proconsular way in which he dismissed the opinion of local leaders. Opposition was in fact so strong that towards the end of 1921 Lenin admitted that the project was premature and that the ground must first be prepared by a propaganda campaign among the population.[1] The conflict was intensified between the representative of the Moscow Central Committee, vigorously supported by Stalin —whose political weight had been increasing since he had taken over the post of Gensek—and the Georgian *tsekisty*, since they too had a strong supporter in the person of Makharadze, a distinguished member of the Tseka, who until recently had been in favor of the Zakkraykom. Makharadze was well known for his internationalism, which had led him in the past to oppose the principle of the self-determination of nations so dear to Lenin; he could not easily be accused of "nationalist deviation," a charge that Stalin and Ordzhonikidze were constantly leveling at the Georgians.

The Georgians sabotaged as best they could the measures taken by Ordzhonikidze to bring about the economic integration of the three republics. They installed military guards on the frontiers of the Georgian Republic, demanded residence permits, etc.[2] While Ordzhonikidze was preparing to

---

[1] The national problem and the relation between Soviet Russia and the Caucasian republics are dealt with in detail by Richard Pipes, *The Formation of the Soviet Union: Communism and Nationalism, 1917–1923* (Cambridge, Mass., Harvard University Press, 1954), Chaps. 5 and 6.

[2] Fotieva, *Iz Vospominaniy*, p. 54.

return to the attack, the Georgians passed solemn resolutions, first by their revolutionary military committee, then by their republic's Congress of Soviets, on the inviolability of their national independence—resolutions whose antifederationist character was quite blatant. Nevertheless, in March 1922, Ordzhonikidze, defying the Georgian opposition and depending on the more docile leaders of Armenia and Azerbaijan, announced plans for a federal constitution, which, while promising to safeguard the sovereignty of the Republics, would establish a federal government. The tension between Stalin and Ordzhonikidze on the one hand and the Georgian *tsekisty* on the other mounted still further. The representatives of Moscow declared in their speeches that the nationalist tendencies of the Georgian *tsekisty* should be obliterated "with a branding iron."[3]

This obstinate and eventful struggle continued throughout 1922 and its reverberations often reached Moscow. It was the most serious but not the only affair to arise from the difficult system of relations between the Republics at a time when the Soviet state was beginning to take up her position on the international scene. As a result the leaders were induced to clarify the whole system of the country's national policy. On August 10, 1922, the Politburo called upon the Orgburo to form a commission that would prepare, for the next meeting of the Central Committee, a plan for the regularization of relations between the Russian Federation and the other republics. Lenin was ill and less and less in control of affairs. The leaders were obviously impatient and perhaps already had a clear idea of the conclusions they were going to reach, for the commission was formed the day after the Politburo's decision. Its composition is not without interest. It

[3] *Ibid.*

included Stalin, Kuibyshev, Ordzhonikidze, Rakovsky, Sokolnikov, and probably also Molotov (who presided at one of the sessions) as representatives of the Russian government; and representing the Republics, Agamaly-Ogly (Azerbaijan), Myasnikov (Armenia), Mdivani (Georgia), Petrovsky (Ukraine) and Cherviakov (Byelorussia).[4]

At the head of the commission was of course Stalin, as Commissar for the Nationalities—he was to retain this post for about another year. From his powerful position as Gensek he could now influence the composition of the commissions set up by the Politburo. In fact, it can be seen that this particular commission was dominated by his political allies, and Stalin himself drew up the resolution of the commission on the mutual relations between the RSFSR and the independent Republics. This resolution, known as the "autonomization plan," provided for the inclusion of these "independent Republics" in the Russian Federation as "autonomous Republics." The plan also stipulated that the government of the Russian Federation, its VTSIK (Central Executive Committee) and its Sovnarkom would henceforth constitute the government of the whole group of Republics.[5]

The text of Stalin's plan was sent for approval to the Party Central Committees of the Republics; it was approved by Azerbaijan and Armenia, now in the hands of safe men, but objected to elsewhere. The Byelorussian Central Committee replied that it would prefer the present system of relations based on bilateral treaties. According to our sources, the Ukraine did not take up a definite position, but we are not told why.[6] The reply of the Georgians was categorical: they

---

[4] According to the notes of the Institute of Marxism-Leninism published in *Soch.*, Vol. XLV, pp. 556-60.

[5] Stalin's plan is reproduced in Appendix I.

[6] *Soch.*, Vol. XLV, p. 556.

were against the plan. A session of their Central Committee, held on September 15, decided "to consider premature the unification of the independent Republics on the basis of autonomization, proposed by Comrade Stalin's theses. We regard the unification of economic endeavor and of general policy indispensable, but with the retention of all the attributes of independence."[7] This decision, passed with only one dissenting vote, provoked an immediate reply from Ordzhonikidze and his Zakkraykom, who adopted a resolution approving Stalin's plan, and what is more, used its superiority in the Party hierarchy to order the Georgian Central Committee to conform to Stalin's orders and not to make its divergences with Moscow public.[8] Again, according to the same source, it was not the first time that attempts had been made to present the Georgians with a *fait accompli;* it had already been the case when Moscow decided to invade Georgia and depose the Menshevik government without warning the local Communists. Now, even before his plans for autonomization had been discussed, Stalin appears to have sent a telegram to Mdivani on August 29, 1922, informing him that henceforth the decisions of the highest governing bodies of the RSFSR (VTSIK, Sovnarkom and STO—the Council of Labor and Defense) were binding on all the Republics. Such an initiative could not fail to make the Georgians' *nyet* to the whole plan more categorical than ever.

Once the reactions of the Central Committees of the Republics had been assembled by Moscow, the commission met again on September 24 and 25. Stalin's plan was adopted almost in its entirety. There was only one abstention, that of the Georgian delegate, Mdivani. The paragraph-by-paragraph discussion did not cause Stalin and Molotov, the chair-

---

[7] *Ibid.*
[8] Pipes, *Formation of the Soviet Union,* pp. 271–72.

men at alternate meetings, much more trouble. Only the second paragraph, stipulating that the government of the Russian Federation would become the government of all the Republics, met with any opposition: the abstention of the Ukrainian delegate, Petrovsky, and an opposing vote from Mdivani. In fact, this success was more apparent than real; the true feelings of the delegates became clearer during the examination of secondary problems; it is probable that no one wished to defy the representatives of the Political Bureau and Orgburo on the dangerous ground of general principles. But when Petrovsky proposed that the plan should be submitted once more to discussion by the *obkomy,* the regional committees of the Party in the Republics, his amendment, which scarcely concealed his real desire to put off the decision and perhaps even to defeat it, received four votes out of nine, including that of one of Moscow's "unconditionals," Agamaly-Ogly, who now sided with Mdivani, Petrovsky, and Cherviakov. This shows how widespread the opposition of the Republics to autonomization really was; of the six, four at least were in varying degrees against it. Once his motion was rejected, Petrovsky demanded that the minutes of the meeting should contain a statement to the effect that the Ukraine had not yet taken up a position on the plan as a whole. The tactics of the Ukrainians were becoming clear: they did not yet dare or wish to make a frontal attack on Stalin's text. Perhaps they wanted to test the ground and to know more of Lenin's position and of the power relations within the Politburo and Central Committee. But, according to the historian Richard Pipes, on October 3, a few days after the meetings of the commission, their Central Committee voted for the maintenance of relations with the RSFSR on the basis of the proposals of the Frunze commission, that is, independence, the status quo.

Meanwhile Lenin, still convalescing, but keenly interested in the problem, asked Stalin for information on the progress being made in the commission's work. He received this information on September 25; Stalin sent him the whole dossier. Lenin's reaction was not slow in coming. The letter he wrote the following day to Kamenev, his deputy on the Sovnarkom, and not to Stalin directly, drew Kamenev's attention to the importance of the affair and asked him to give considerable thought to this problem. Lenin was not alarmed by the actual events themselves, or by the means already being used to implement the plan. The Georgian conflict did not yet interest him as such, and despite his frequent meetings with all the protagonists in the affair, the impression prevailed that he still tended to trust the information supplied by his friend Ordzhonikidze and by Stalin. Further proof of this will appear the following month. In this letter, Lenin spoke of Mdivani as of someone "suspected of being a *nezavisimets*," that is, a nationalist in the pejorative sense, but he did not formally repeat this accusation, and on the other hand he found Stalin "in rather too much of a hurry."[9] It was therefore for reasons of principle and not of fact that Lenin was led to reject the autonomization plan and to suggest a different solution. We must achieve, he says, "a Federation of Republics enjoying equal rights." In order to guarantee this equality, he deleted from Stalin's plan the paragraph relating to the adhesion of the Republics to the RSFSR, and proposed in its place "a formal union with the RSFSR, in a Union of Soviet Republics of Europe and Asia."

The Russian government would not be that of the Union. Lenin proposed the creation of a Federal Executive Com-

---

[9] Lenin's letter is reproduced in Appendix II.

mittee of the Union of Soviet Republics and a new federal Sovnarkom, an organization that would also include under its jurisdiction the Russian government itself. In this way a project was created that was soon to be known as the USSR. After his letter to Kamenev, which must also have been circulated among the other members of the Politburo, Lenin followed attentively the development of the affair from his country house at Gorki. On September 29 he was visited by Ordzhonikidze and the following day he met the Georgian Central Committee members, Okudzhava, Dumbadze and Minadze, who had been sent to Moscow by the Georgians to oppose Stalin. Lenin may well have disappointed them, but at least he listened to them attentively.

Meanwhile, Stalin was behaving like a very impatient man. Convinced of the correctness of his point of view and determined to establish a *fait accompli*, he did not wait for Lenin's opinion but recommunicated the results of his commission's work to all the members of the Central Committee, to be used as material for their next meeting, which was to take place on October 6. Lenin's letter containing a plan for a Union of the Soviet Republics of Europe and Asia was regarded by Stalin as a useless piece of interference on the part of the "old man" in a field in which he, the Commissar for the Nationalities, had acquired a sound reputation; meanwhile, he was making sure that things would progress without hitch, despite the shortsighted activities of the Georgian troublemakers. Stalin was irritated but not impressed by Lenin's intervention, Stalin and Kamenev, probably at one of the meetings of the Politburo, exchanged two brief notes on the subject of Lenin's memorandum.

Kamenev's note reads: "Ilich is going to war to defend independence."

Stalin replied: "I think we should be firm with Lenin."[10]

Which is what, departing from his usual prudence, he then did. On September 27, he communicated the text of Lenin's memorandum to the members of the Politburo, appending a letter in which he made no secret of his opinion and accused the head of the Sovnarkom quite openly of "national liberalism" and of encouraging the separatists. Here is an extract from this letter, part of which is available to us:

"Paragraph 2. Lenin's correction to paragraph 2, proposing to create, along with the All-Russian Central Executive Committee of the RSFSR, a Central Executive Committee of the Federation should not, in my opinion, be adopted. The existence of two Central Executive Committees in Moscow, one of which will obviously represent a 'lower house' and the other an 'upper' house will give us nothing but conflict and debate. . . .

"Paragraph 4. On the subject of paragraph 4, in my opinion, comrade Lenin himself 'hurried' a little, demanding a fusion of the Commissariats of Finance, Food Supply, Labor and National Economy with the commissariats of the Federation. There is hardly a doubt that this 'hurriedness' will 'supply fuel to the advocates of independence,' to the detriment of the national liberalism of comrade Lenin.

"Paragraph 5. Comrade Lenin's correction of paragraph 5 is, in my opinion, superfluous."[11]

Stalin hits back at Lenin point by point, often falling into glibness and demagogy. Lenin's moderate charge that Stalin was being rather too impatient is flung back at him, and by accusing Lenin of "national liberalism" Stalin is adding an

[10] P. N. Pospelov *et al., Vladimir Ilich Lenin, Biografia,* 2d ed. (Moscow, Gospolitizdat, 1963), p. 611.

[11] This letter is reproduced by Trotsky in *The Stalin School of Falsification,* pp. 66–67. The Marxist-Leninist Institute in Moscow does not reproduce it but confirms its existence and Stalin's accusations against Lenin of "national liberalism."

attack on general principles. But he does not stop there; anticipating Lenin's counterattacks, he declares him guilty of an overhasty centralism, which is exactly the opposite of the supposed "national liberalism." In a sense the whole of Stalin is contained in this letter. One can see from his way of arguing that for him tactics outweigh any other consideration. So much so that he did not consider it necessary to defend for more than one day opinions that he had presented nonetheless so trenchantly. Realizing that he would find himself in a minority in the Central Committee, he gave in all along the line and transformed his autonomization plan into a plan of union, incorporating Lenin's amendments. The new text, signed by Stalin, Molotov, Ordzhonikidze and Myasnikov, was sent to the members of the Central Committee without any mention of its differences from the previous plan. The editors of Volume XLV of Lenin's *Works* say that these differences were "glossed over." The introduction to the new plan claims quite imperturbably that it is merely "a slightly modified, more precise formulation" of that of the Orgburo, which had been "correct in principle and fully acceptable."[12]

It is not known whether Lenin read Stalin's letter or the preamble to the project as reformulated by the Gensek. He did not take part in the meeting of the Central Committee which, on October 6, ratified the new version. But curiously enough, on the day of the meeting, acting on an impulse of whose cause we know nothing, he sent a brief note to Kamenev which was to be made public only fifteen years later. Lenin wrote, not without a touch of humor:

"Comrade Kamenev! I declare war to the death on dominant-nation chauvinism. I shall eat it with all my healthy

[12] *Soch.*, Vol. XLV, p. 559. The text of the final resolutions is reproduced in Appendix III.

teeth as soon as I get rid of this accursed bad tooth. It must
be *absolutely* insisted that the Union Central Executive Committee should be *presided over* in turn by a

Russian,

Ukrainian

Georgian, etc.

Absolutely!

Yours,

LENIN"[13]

Thanks to Lenin's authority, his views appeared to be accepted by everybody. The Central Committee adopted the
project in its entirety, entrusting to a new commission the
task of drawing up a more detailed version for the next session. Mdivani did not oppose it, but he demanded that
Georgia, like the Ukraine and Byelorussia, should be admitted to the Union as a separate member and not as part of a
Transcaucasian Federation, as Ordzhonikidze and Stalin
continued to demand. In fact, Stalin and Ordzhonikidze were
pursuing a personal vendetta in which they had fully committed themselves; for these two Georgians it was a question
of being proved right while other Georgians were proved
wrong, and Lenin's silence on this particular point merely
encouraged them. The Georgians protested once again to
Moscow against the Transcaucasian Federation, only to receive from Stalin the harsh reply that the Central Committee
had unanimously rejected their protests.[14] A new and more
violent wave of protests then arose from secret and sometimes
even from public meetings in which the Georgians never
ceased to proclaim and reaffirm their independence.

Ordzhonikidze now began to employ stronger methods.

[13] *Ibid.*, p. 214.
[14] Pipes, *Formation of the Soviet Union*, p. 274.

With the backing of the Moscow Secretariat, which he constantly enjoyed, he ordered the supporters of the Georgian Central Committee to leave their country and, as a disciplinary measure, place themselves at the disposal of the Central Committee in Moscow.[15] When, on their return from the capital, where they had been following the development of the affair on behalf of the Georgian Central Committee, the three representatives sent by this republic made their report, the Georgian Central Committee confirmed by a large majority its determination to join the Union as a separate entity. At the same time Makharadze and Tsintsadze sent private letters to Bukharin and Kamenev, hoping in this way to short-circuit Stalin's action. They were soon disabused: it turned out that Bukharin and Kamenev supported the Secretariat. They responded with new accusations of nationalism and insisted that the Georgians should submit to Party discipline. An even more bitter disappointment awaited the Georgians. When Bukharin conveyed their complaint to Lenin, Lenin, who could not yet see the contradiction between his "Unionist" principles—his determination to combat Great Russian chauvinism and the policy practiced toward Georgia—replied at once with a cold, rather irritated telegram:

"21/10/22

TBILISI, to the CC of the CPG, Tsintsadze and Kavtaradze (copies to the member of the Central Committee Ordzhonikidze and to the Secretary of the Zakkraykom Orakhelashvili).

Astonished at the unseemly tone of the note, communicated by telegram, signed by Tsintsadze and others, which

---

[15] Fotieva, *Iz Vospominaniy*, p. 49.

has been conveyed to me, why nobody knows, by Bukharin and not by one of the secretaries of the Central Committee, I was under the impression that all divergences had been thoroughly dealt with by the resolutions of the plenum of the Central Committee, with my indirect participation and the direct participation of Mdivani. Consequently, I firmly condemn the invectives addressed to Ordzhonikidze and insist that your conflict, conducted in a more seemly and loyal tone, should be settled by the Secretariat of the CC of the RCP to which I am conveying your declaration by telegram.

> Respectfully yours,
> SIGNED: LENIN"[16]

Lenin was so certain of the value of his information on the affair that he placed the complaint against Ordzhonikidze and Stalin in the hands of . . . Stalin!

Their patience exhausted, despairing of obtaining any justice in Moscow and exasperated by the "deportations" ordered by Ordzhonikidze, the Georgian *tsekisty* made an unprecedented gesture: on October 22, they resigned collectively.[17] This was no doubt just what Ordzhonikidze had been hoping for. His Zakkraykom immediately appointed a new Central Committee consisting of incompetent but docile young men who accepted the Federation without batting an eyelid. The Moscow Secretariat had hastened to accept the resignation of the former *tsekisty* and the new appointments. But the abscess had not yet been drained. The members of the old Central Committee did not give up the struggle. The change of leadership merely served to emphasize the unpopularity of Ordzhonikidze in his own country. This irritated

---

[16] *Soch.*, Vol. LIV, pp. 299–300.

[17] Fotieva, *Iz Vospominaniy*, p. 52. In fact, nine of the eleven members of the Georgian Central Committee resigned.

him considerably, especially as the concrete measures taken to implement the Federation were progressing too slowly for his liking, sabotaged as they were by the partisans of Georgian independence. Incidents, intrigues and complaints to Moscow multiplied.

In the course of one of these confrontations Ordzhonikidze lost his temper and struck another Party member, a supporter of Mdivani. The incident took place at a private session held at Ordzhonikidze's. Rykov, Lenin's deputy and a member of the Politburo, was present.[18] The "fiery Sergo" (Ordzhonikidze) thought he was invulnerable. But this time a request to Moscow to reopen the inquiry, signed by Makharadze and others, could no longer be ignored.[19] While persisting in their defense of the Zakkraykom's line as "correct in principle" and attacking "the essentially incorrect positions" of the Georgian Central Committee, which they refer to in their commentary as the "Mdivani group," the editors of the latest edition of Lenin's *Works* enumerate nonetheless an impressive list of "errors committed by Ordzhonikidze": "He showed that he lacked the flexibility and prudence necessary for the conduct of the Party's national policy in Georgia; he allowed bureaucratic methods; he took certain measures too rapidly; he did not always take into account the opinions and rights of the Central Committee of the Communist Party of Georgia. Moreover he showed that he lacked the self-control necessary in his relations with the Mdivani group."[20]

At this point Lenin was beginning to get anxious about the situation. He was suddenly alarmed by a letter from Okudzhava, a member of the old Georgian Central Com-

[18] *Ibid.*, p. 75. The incident probably took place towards the end of November.
[19] *Ibid.*, p. 52.
[20] *Soch.*, Vol. XLV, p. 595.

mittee, accusing Ordzhonikidze of making threats against the Georgian Communists.[21] When the Politburo sent him for his vote the names of the members of the commission of inquiry that the Secretariat was sending to Georgia to settle the dispute within the Party there, Lenin, as we read in the "Journal" for November 24, preferred to abstain. We do not know whether he intended in this way to express some doubt as to the impartiality of the commission, whose three members—Dzerzhinsky, Lozovsky and Kapsukas-Mitskevitchius —had been proposed by Stalin, but it is clear at least that he had become suspicious of his first informants and was seeking other sources of information on which to base an opinion. Rykov went to Georgia, either because Lenin had sent him there or for some other reason. In any case he too must have been following the affair and consulting with Lenin about it. Lenin himself awaited the return of the commission and of Rykov with increasing impatience. The secretaries note faithfully in the "Journal" his incessant questions on their itineraries.

At this stage in the development of the affair, a few general remarks might be made. We are no longer presented with a simple and inevitable divergence in the execution of a policy between principles and aims on the one hand and methods of application on the other. These methods, taken as a whole, were now the expression of a change of objective that had occurred often unconsciously in the minds of certain of the leaders: centralism in the state had been erected into a supreme principle. Ordzhonikidze was behaving like a governor general, flouting legal and statutory considerations, using brute force against the Communists of the national republics, doing in fact everything that his opponents within

<hr />

[21] Pipes, *Formation of the Soviet Union*, p. 281.

the Party, and often paradoxically the Stalinists themselves, included under the critical term of *administrirovanie*. These practices were congealing into a system whose rationale did not stem from the aspirations of the October Revolution. While advocating prudence, circumspection and flexibility, above all in the handling of the difficult national problem, Lenin directed a dictatorship that could only survive if it were implacable. It is hardly surprising that he should have helped in appointing leaders who were capable of overcoming opposition; he himself had sent Ordzhonikidze into the Caucasus as a conqueror. Among the delegates and commissars, front commanders and regional secretaries that had participated in the struggle of the civil war and its immediate aftermath were to be found two of the great categories of militants of which the Party leadership was composed. The first of these were the intellectuals and idealists, sensitive to doctrinal requirements and deeply attached to their vision of socialism; most of them had come to the Party through contact with Western Marxism, particularly in the course of long stays in Europe during the emigration. The second group were primarily executives, men of action, practitioners of the revolution, more concerned with day-to-day realities; by training and ability they were seldom intellectuals; they were generally former underground Bolsheviks who had not known the experience of emigration.

Both kinds of men had had a role to play in the Revolution, the civil war and the implementation of Lenin's ideals. But the course of events, which turned out to be more tragic and more painful than the theoreticians had foreseen, soon favored a predominance of activists of the stamp of Ordzhonikidze, Kaganovich, Molotov, Kuibyshev or Stalin, rather than men like Rakovsky, Krestinsky, Serebryakov, Preobrazhensky, Makharadze and Trotsky. The terrible logic of

Russian realities drove some to catastrophic ends, while promising a long reign to others—though many of these were to be eliminated in the great purges of 1936–1938. Isaac Deutscher suggests a distinction between those Bolsheviks who remained attached to the dream and those who were more concerned with power. In the process of realizing the dream, deeper and deeper dilemmas appeared and the cleavage between the two types of men became increasingly obvious.[22]

Lenin's own personality was in a way a successful synthesis of the two types of character; he was capable of linking an idealistic fidelity to the principles of doctrine with a pragmatism that preserved him from a utopian or conservative rigidity of doctrine. It was this that constituted both his strength and his weakness; it was also the source of his mental torments; it enabled him to work with Trotsky while at the same time giving the highest responsibilities to Stalin. Stalin's ascendancy was forged during the civil war and the period of Lenin's illness. In spite of appearances and the fact that the country hardly knew him—whereas Trotsky was immensely popular—Stalin had become under Lenin a leader of the first order; Lenin recognized him as such. This is particularly apparent in the letter on the constitution of the USSR, written to Kamenev on September 26, in which Lenin congratulates himself on having won a concession from Stalin on a paragraph of the draft version. A study of the "Testament" confirms this.

During the year 1922 Lenin saw Stalin a good deal and spoke with him at great length on each occasion. His confidence in Stalin is proved by the fact that in the matter of the Georgian dispute he backed him against Mdivani's group for

[22] Deutscher, *The Prophet Unarmed*, p. 73.

a whole year, despite his personal dealings with their representatives. But the deep differences between Lenin and Stalin are apparent in their respective attitudes to the national question. Stalin proposed a simple, expeditious solution that would crystallize and strengthen the real organ of power. Wasn't the government of the RSFSR for all practical purposes also the government of the other Republics? Very well, then, it would become the government of the whole Union officially. How would this be done? The answer lies in paragraph 6 of Stalin's project: "If the present decision is confirmed by the Central Committee of the RCP, it will not be made public, but communicated to the Central Committees of the Republics for circulation among the Soviet organs, the Central Executive Committees or the Congresses of the Soviets of the said Republics before the convocation of the All-Russian Congress of the Soviets, where it will be declared to be the wish of these Republics."[23] Since in any case it was the Central Committee in Moscow that had decided and imposed its decision on the national Central Committees by a "general directive," that is, by an order, failure to implement which was punishable by disciplinary measures, and since the will of the Central Committee was later to be solemnly declared as the wish of the Republics, the significance of Stalin's project is quite clear: it was a question of translating a *de facto* situation into a *de jure* one. Lenin on the other hand refused to confine his attention exclusively to considerations of administrative efficiency and sought a solution to the problem by applying principles that he had developed over many years. He says in his letter—and there is no reason to doubt his sincerity—that he wishes not to destroy the independence of the Soviet Republics but to

[23] *Soch.*, Vol. XLV, p. 558.

create a new stage in the constitutional hierarchy, "a Federation of independent Republics." Lenin was also concerned with efficiency, of course, and the solution adopted must also strengthen the state, but for him the whole problem of the nationalities had to be solved and not suppressed. Internationalism must not be sacrificed to centralism; it was also necessary to combat the strong tradition of oppression that had characterized the Tsarist state. This determination to bear constantly in mind the principles of socialist ideology finds its expression in Lenin's project for a union, in which due consideration is given to the federal character of the Union, the rights of the Republics, the preservation of their independence and their individual susceptibilities. The institutions he proposed were to act as a guarantee against the encroaching power of the predominant nation. For this project to be realizable in Soviet conditions it was necessary for the Central Committee in Moscow to have the will, the conviction and the power to make sure that the proposed institutions and guarantees did not in fact remain a dead letter, whatever pressure was brought to bear to the contrary. It was also necessary that the Republics and above all the local Communists should be able to defend their point of view within the Party, legally and institutionally, without incurring the risk of falling immediately under attack for "factional activities" or "infractions against discipline." If Lenin's proposals were to have any meaning, changes would have to be made in the internal organization of the Party. We shall see later how and to what extent Lenin envisaged such changes.

For his part, Stalin was sincere in claiming that the new version of the project of union differed only in certain details from his own original project, which as he said was also "correct in principle and absolutely acceptable." He was convinced, in fact, that in the course of events the real interests of the state would gain the upper hand and that the Union would function in any case as he had expected it to. In these circumstances he saw no reason why he should not give in to Lenin completely, on paper. In any case, for him there was no divorce between the principles and the practice of the Bolshevik program. Lenin, on the other hand, became increasingly aware of such a distortion, realized that he was partly responsible for it and that he must prevent things from moving too far away from his original intention.

5

THE SICK MAN AND THE WATCHER

When Lenin resumed the conduct of affairs in October 1922 he had recovered neither his capacity for work nor his former grip. His speech of November 20 (his last public appearance) is confused and quite obviously improvised. He touched on the subjects that most worried him, but anxious not to sow panic, he tried to comfort his audience by offering solutions. Nevertheless, there was a lack of any clear view of the future. The NEP was necessary but dangerous; it was not yet sufficiently under control and people had not yet got used to it: "This change of direction continues to cause us certain difficulties—I would go so far as to say considerable difficulties." And again: "Extraordinary measures must be taken, extraordinary discoveries made."[1] It was true that the regime had effected a retreat, but it must now reorganize its forces and return to the attack; however, it was not known by what means this was to be done. The general situation was disastrous: "We are living in the conditions of a state so ruined by war, so completely deflected from its normal course, and so weakened by its sufferings that we must, in spite of ourselves, make our calculations by taking as our point of comparison an extremely weak rate, that of before the war."

Foreign aid would be slow in coming, and the speech shows a Lenin sadly divided between the desire to safeguard all the achievements and even all the hopes of the past— those of the October days and those too, real or illusory, of the civil war—and the realization that it might be necessary to retreat still further, without losing either hope or power. The reconciliation of ends and means was not easy. With the NEP, everything had to be learned over again: "It is in order to make such a study possible that it seems to me the time has come to assure each other firmly of one thing: in effecting this retreat, which we have called the New Economic Policy, we have done things in such a way that while abandoning no new acquisition, we can offer the capitalists such advantages that any state, however hostile to us, would be forced to accept markets and relations with us."

Lenin knew that this looked very like a wager: the Communists had not yet learned the practice of public affairs, and rather than dominating the administrative machine they were themselves dominated by it. The only thing that Lenin was able to say with any conviction was that "the NEP continues

[1] *Soch.*, Vol. XLV, p. 302.

to be the principal, immediate, universal imperative of the present day."[2]

Yet this new orientation had not yet been given a definitive formulation; nothing had been definitively achieved.

A few days after this speech, when Lenin was beginning to be troubled by the gravest suspicions about the Georgian affair, his doctors insisted that he should do much less work. Lenin was a difficult patient; he did not take kindly to inactivity, but he was forced to admit that his physical strength was declining. In the end, he agreed to go to his country home at Gorki near Moscow and rest, but he continued to take an active part in political life by letter and telephone. He waited impatiently for news of Rykov and Dzerzhinsky, who were expected to return soon from the Caucasus, but he devoted most of his time to organizing the work of his deputies in the government, who were now three in number: Rykov, Kamenev and Tsyurupa. He remained constantly in touch with them over their collective plan to redefine the scope of the activities of the Sovnarkom. The reorganization of the Sovnarkom with a new division of responsibilities was obviously linked in his mind with the problem of the succession. At the beginning of December Lenin asked Trotsky to come and see him again. In the course of the conversation he suggested that a "bloc against bureaucracy" should be formed and that Trotsky should join a special committee whose purpose would be to lead such a struggle. Lenin also suggested that Trotsky should become one of his deputies in the government. On this occasion, Trotsky expressed his long-held conviction—it was probably the basis of his previous criticisms of the Workers' and Peasants' Inspection which at the time had so irritated Lenin—that the struggle against bu-

[2] *Ibid.,* p. 308.

reaucracy should begin with the elimination of the evil from among those most likely to foster it, namely the Party, and more particularly the Party leadership.[3] Lenin, more aware and less confident than before, soon adopted Trotsky's idea and drew several conclusions from it.

Rykov returned at last from Georgia and reported back to Lenin on December 9, 1922.[4] The "Journal" merely mentions this meeting, and we do not know what Rykov said. Three days later Dzerzhinsky also returned, and Lenin left Gorki for Moscow in order to confer with him. Dzerzhinsky's inquiry naturally corroborated the explanations originally provided by the Secretariat. Ordzhonikidze was whitewashed and all the blame laid once again on the dangerous deviationists. But this time Lenin was more aware of what was going on, and he suspected a lie beneath the scaffolding of the official thesis. He was particularly struck by two facts that Dzerzhinsky was unable to conceal. First, the commission had decided to recall to Moscow the leaders of the former Georgian Central Committee, who were held responsible for everything. Secondly, Ordzhonikidze had lost his temper and had gone so far as to strike an opponent, also a member of the Party. Fotieva recounts, and Lenin himself confirms, that Dzerzhinsky's account "upset him deeply."[5] The "Journal" shows how much this incident preoccupied Lenin throughout his illness.

One might wonder if there were not something rather ridiculous in attributing so much importance to an expres-

---

[3] See Trotsky's account of this conversation in *The Stalin School of Falsification*, pp. 73–74, and Deutscher, *The Prophet Unarmed*, pp. 66, 68–69. Once again Trotsky refused to become Lenin's deputy, but with less conviction than before. Concerning Trotsky's earlier criticisms of the RKI and the Gosplan, see *Soch.*, Vol. XLV, pp. 180–82.

[4] Pipes, *Formation of the Soviet Union*, p. 281.

[5] Fotieva, *Iz Vospominaniy*, p. 54, and *Soch.*, Vol. XLV, p. 596.

sion of irritation on the part of a Party leader engaged in overcoming the difficulties of executing a policy that had been laid down for him, in a country that had only just emerged from mass bloodshed and famine. No doubt Ordzhonikidze's comrades-in-arms and accomplices within the Secretariat thought so. But for Lenin the image of a Communist governor behaving like a satrap in a conquered country was an indication, a disturbing symptom of the sickness that had struck at the entire body politic and of the damage it could still do. The intricacies of the Georgian affair suddenly appeared to him in a different light. On December 30, 1922, he wrote: "If matters have come to such a pass . . . we can imagine what a mess we have got ourselves into." The meeting with Dzerzhinsky had a detrimental effect on Lenin's illness and probably hastened his attack. He must have had a disturbed night; on the morning of December 13, two serious attacks forced him to give up work completely.

The two days devoted to the return of the dossiers were still fairly busy for him. He continued his correspondence with his deputies about the organization of the work of the Sovnarkom; he received a few people with whose help he hoped to have the Central Committee's decision on foreign trade reversed; he exchanged letters with Trotsky and entrusted to him, as we have seen, the defense of their common cause. After another night of insomnia, Lenin had another very serious attack on the morning of December 16. Nevertheless, he hurried to dictate a last note to his assistants before the doctors arrived. There was now no hope that he would be able to take part in the next Congress of the Soviets, for which he had been preparing for weeks. He was confined to his small room in the Kremlin: it was impossible to take him to Gorki as originally intended because he was unable to travel. However, the fact that he remained in the Kremlin

was to have considerable importance in the activities of the
sick man during the eighty days still left to him of intellectual
lucidity. Visits were forbidden: he was to see only his wife
Krupskaya, his sister Maria Ilinichna and three or four secretaries, apart of course from the medical staff. His entourage
were forbidden to communicate with him or to inform him of
current state affairs, in order "not to give him any cause for
reflection or concern."[6] Thus began Lenin's exhausting
struggle to be kept informed of what interested him, to
formulate his opinions and to communicate them to the
right people. This was not the caprice of a sick man who,
refusing to face death, continued to act as if nothing had
happened. On the contrary, Lenin knew that he might die at
any moment and leave the country and the Party in an extremely difficult situation, without a clear program of action,
without even any positive indications of the direction to be
followed; he felt that he must say at least the essential things
about the more urgent problems, that it was the duty of the
head of state, of the leader of an unprecedented revolution,
to do so. It was thought that the patient's state would be
worsened by political cares, but it was worse for the head of
state not to be able to do as much as was humanly possible
towards the completion of his task.

The ambiguity of the situation was further increased by
the fact that the man chosen to make sure the doctors' orders
were scrupulously carried out was none other than Stalin.[7]
The actual orders were given by the doctors, but in close con-
sultation with the supervisor appointed by the Central Committee. Stalin was officially instructed to keep himself in-

[6] *Soch.*, Vol. XLV, p. 710.
[7] By a decision of the Central Committee on December 18, 1922 (*ibid.*,
p. 608).

formed of everything that happened at Lenin's bedside. He applied himself zealously to the task. A significant incident that took place between Krupskaya and Stalin throws some light on the way in which he intended to carry out his mission.

On December 22, learning from his informers that the previous day Krupskaya had written a letter, in fact a brief note, under Lenin's dictation, Stalin telephoned her and, as Krupskaya herself says, piled "unworthy abuse and threats" upon her.[8] He even threatened to have her prosecuted by the Party Central Control Commission for disobeying the doctors' orders. Such indelicacy was unprecedented in the relations between the Party leaders and Lenin's family. There was obviously no reason to doubt Krupskaya's devotion to the patient and her ability to nurse him. Stalin's action was not even justified in principle: Krupskaya had obtained the permission of the doctor then treating her husband—and Stalin could easily have verified this. He had abandoned all considerations of prudence and tact because he was acting in a violent fit of anger: the letter written by Krupskaya at Lenin's dictation was the one addressed to Trotsky congratulating him for having triumphed "without a blow being struck" in the Central Committee's discussion on the foreign trade monopoly. Stalin was perfectly well aware that relations between Lenin and Trotsky had recently become increasingly close. He had not been much concerned about this during 1922, for the two leaders, while never in conflict on points of principle, had perpetually engaged in skirmishes on current questions. This did not prevent Lenin from sug-

---

[8] Krupskaya's letter to Kamenev is reproduced, apparently with some cuts, in *Soch.*, Vol. LIV, pp. 674–75. See Appendix V.

gesting to Trotsky that he should become his deputy, but
Trotsky had refused, and on this occasion Stalin had succeeded, not without a certain malicious satisfaction, in getting
the Politburo to censure Trotsky for failure of duty.[9] It was
only later that the *entente cordiale* on the monopoly question
came into being.

Moreover, on November 25 Lenin, as we have recently
learned,[10] informed the Politburo that he approved of
Trotsky's proposals on the use of tactics in connection with
the International; above all, in the second part of this message, he expressed a very flattering opinion of Trotsky's
theses concerning the NEP—he even insisted that they
should be published as a pamphlet and widely distributed.
It was undoubtedly a great compliment, for they concerned
one of the most complicated problems of Soviet policy and
one that had caused Lenin a good deal of worry. It is hardly
surprising then that Stalin, more concerned than anybody
with the problem of the succession, should have exploded
with indignation on learning of this new mark of esteem conferred on Trotsky by Lenin, especially as he was beginning
to fear that the *rapprochement* between the two men would
be accompanied by a positive campaign against himself. This
is why Stalin did all in his power to strengthen still further
his supervision of Lenin. Evidence of this is a telephone call
made to one of Lenin's closest collaborators, his chief secretary, Fotieva. This time the tone of the communication was
polite enough. On January 30 Fotieva notes in the "Journal":
"Stalin asked if I was not saying too much to Vladimir Ilich.
How does he manage to keep informed about current business? For example, his article on the Workers' and Peasants'

[9] Deutscher, *The Prophet Unarmed*, p. 61.
[10] *Soch.*, Vol. LIV, p. 314.

Inspection shows that he knew of certain circumstances." This was yet another subject by means of which a personal attack was being made against Stalin, in a somewhat veiled way no doubt, but one that was obvious enough to Stalin himself.

It was against such close supervision and such strict limitations on his activities—legally covered, of course—that Lenin had to struggle. An example of this occurred on December 23. He had suffered a severe attack of his illness during the night of December 22–23, but had been able to sleep. Nevertheless, he realized the next morning that once again a part of his body, his right hand and leg, was paralyzed. The news was communicated at once to the Politburo. Despite the commotion caused by this attack, Lenin's thoughts were still preoccupied with the future of the state and Party. He then asked for permission to dictate for five minutes each day. He felt that the moment when he would have to "leave the ranks" might come at any time and if he did not dictate, "when a problem worried him, he could not sleep." When permission was given, Lenin called one of his secretaries and dictated about thirty lines in four minutes. He felt ill; the doctors were told and remained within call. The next day he demanded the right to continue what he called his "journal." The doctors tried to stop him, but Lenin presented them with an ultimatum: if he was not allowed to dictate for a few minutes a day he would refuse to co-operate with the doctors at all.[11] A council consisting of doctors and members of the Politburo, Stalin, Bukharin and Kamenev, did not see how they could act otherwise. Permission was granted, but the Politburo's decision laid it

---

[11] The account of Ulyanova, Lenin's sister, reproduced in *Soch.*, Vol. XLV, p. 591.

down that the notes should not be in the form of correspondence that necessitated a reply.[12] It was in this way, then, that
the "Testament" was written, at first a series of very brief
notes, dictated at the cost of enormous effort for a few minutes each day. But Lenin's robust constitution seemed to
perform a miracle. His health began to improve and there
were even hopes for a cure. He was later able to dictate for
three quarters of an hour each day and even read and continue the struggle through his faithful entourage—his wife,
his sister and his secretaries, all deeply devoted to him.

The "Testament" in the strict sense of the term consists of
notes dictated between December 23 and 31, with a supple-
ment dated January 4. In the *Works* these notes are called
"Letter to the Congress." But the real expression of Lenin's
ideas, the testament in the true sense of the term, is to be
found in all the writings of this period. There is no question
that one can find in these writings a coherent view of the
international situation both present and future, important
elements of a program and line of action, and an attempt to
elucidate the probable course of internal development. Apart
from the notes, these ideas are developed in five articles written in January and February 1923, although a majority
of the Politburo had made attempts to prevent or delay their
appearance.[13] Time for reflection, dictation (sometimes in
two versions), corrections, preliminary study, documenta-
tion, detailed reading of works on history, economics, socialism, Marxism and agrarian problems—all his activities were

[12] *Ibid.,* p. 710. See Appendix VI.
[13] Lenin's notes are to be found in Vol. XXXVI of the fourth edition
in English of his works, and the articles in Vol. XXXIII. The work
schedule and the last article are reproduced in our Appendix VII and
Appendix IX. The notes and articles appear in Vol. XLV of the fifth
edition of the *Works,* and several previously unpublished letters are
included in Vol. LIV.

prearranged in a plan of work. As soon as his health had improved a little, Lenin dictated a work schedule that he finally succeeded in completing almost entirely.[14] His illness had not impaired his lucidity, but his increasing physical weakness inevitably affected the speed with which he developed his thoughts and sometimes the clarity of his writing, especially in the first, all too brief dictations.

[14] This schedule is reproduced in *Soch.*, Vol. XLV, p. 592. See Appendix VII.

6

LENIN'S
"TESTAMENT"

The notes that Lenin began to dictate on December 23 were
intended—it is clear from the first line—as a proposal to the
next Party Congress that "a number of changes be made in
our political system."[1] He then enumerated extremely con-
cisely the reasons that led him to propose these changes. As
the class struggle became sharper on the international plane,
the country's leadership would probably be confronted by a
series of unfavorable events. The unity of the Central Com-

[1] *Soch.*, Vol. XLV, p. 343. Concerning the English translation, see
Chapter 5, note 13.

mittee must therefore be strengthened. Only then would it be capable of carrying out the urgent task of reorganizing, or rather rebuilding, the state apparatus, and at the same time preventing the Party from succumbing to its most immediate danger: a split that could lead to struggles between groups and personalities. According to Lenin, it was the danger to the stability of the Party that must be regarded as the most urgent problem.

The first step to take was to increase quite considerably the size of the Central Committee. This would have the effect of increasing the stability of the Party "a thousandfold." Lenin also proposed "to invest the decisions of the State Planning Commission with legislative force, meeting in this respect the wishes of Comrade Trotsky—to a certain extent and on certain conditions."[2] These ideas can only be understood in the context of Lenin's plan as a whole, but what concerns us here is the part played by the notes in the relations between the leaders.

It has recently been learned that the first note, dated December 23, was sent off at once to Stalin for circulation among the members of the Politburo. Stalin probably showed it to no one.[3] There could be no doubt about the significance of this note as evidence of the *rapprochement* with Trotsky: it concerned a subject (the Gosplan) that had been a matter of dispute between Lenin and Trotsky throughout 1922. Other notes followed that might have reassured Stalin if he had seen them. But they were communicated to no one, at least for a time; they were, in Lenin's own words, "categorically secret."[4]

[2] *Ibid.*

[3] *Ibid.*, pp. 593–94.

[4] *Ibid.*, pp. 592–93. Five copies of the notes were to be made—one for the secret archives, one for Lenin himself, three for Krupskaya—and put

The most serious divergences and the split that might result—the enemies of the regime were right to expect such a split—could have two causes. One was to be found in the social basis of the regime. The whole system rested on an alliance between workers and peasants; if the alliance broke up, "all talk about the stability of our CC would be futile." But such an occurrence was distant and improbable. The more immediate danger lay in the personal relations within the leadership. "The greater part of the danger of a split," which Lenin saw as highly probable, depended on the relations between Stalin and Trotsky. After proceeding to this prophetic judgment, Lenin sketches portraits of six of the leaders: Stalin and Trotsky, Zinoviev and Kamenev, Bukharin and Pyatakov. These notes, written on December 23 and 24, at a time when Lenin's health was giving cause for alarm, bear the mark of a painful effort, through thought and reflection, to elucidate the essential points without jeopardizing by an imprudent word the future continuity and stability of the state and Party.

Of the two youngest men, Bukharin and Pyatakov, one was a brilliant theoretician and extremely popular in the Party, the other was able and strong-willed. But they both had faults. Bukharin's thinking was not entirely Marxist: "there is something scholastic about him (he has never made a study of dialectics, and I think, never fully understood it)." Pyatakov, on the other hand, showed "too much zeal for . . . the administrative side of the work to be relied upon in a serious political matter." However, they were only thirty-

---

in sealed envelopes. These details were revealed by Volodicheva in 1929. Only Lenin had the right to open these envelopes, and after his death, Krupskaya. But Volodicheva did not dare to write the fateful words "after his death" on the envelopes.

four and thirty-two respectively and still had time to correct their faults.

Only a single remark is made about Zinoviev and Kamenev, and its interpretation raises some problems. It concerns their "October episode," when they had opposed Lenin's *coup d'état.* "This was, of course, no accident, but neither can the blame be laid upon them personally, any more than non-Bolshevism can upon Trotsky." What, then, was the purpose of this reference to the past? Was it intended as a warning? Or as an exculpation? Or both? It may be easier to answer this in the light of Lenin's portrait of Stalin and Trotsky, whose conflicting characters might cause a sudden and unintended split in the Party:

"Comrade Stalin, having become Secretary General, has unlimited authority concentrated in his hands, and I am not sure whether he will always be capable of using that authority with sufficient caution. Comrade Trotsky, on the other hand, as his struggle against the CC on the question of the People's Commissariat for Communications has already proved, is distinguished not only by outstanding ability. He is personally perhaps the most capable man in the present CC, but he has displayed excessive self-assurance and shown excessive preoccupation with the purely administrative side of the work."[5]

The very idea that Stalin and Trotsky were the two pre-eminent leaders was, in its placing of Stalin, enough to astonish the country, hurt Trotsky and unpleasantly surprise Zinoviev and Kamenev, who, in the future triumvirate, continued for some years in the belief that they were the strongest. For Lenin, it may well have resulted from his realization of two new factors: the importance of the post of General

[5] *Ibid.,* p. 345.

Secretary, which had only been in existence for eight months, and the fact that the holder of that post had been able to acquire so much power in so short a time. It may also be remarked that the comparison of the two leaders is couched in such terms that no preference is apparent. Trotsky's well-known qualities are counterbalanced by important faults. How serious was his "excessive preoccupation with the purely administrative side of the work"? To answer this question we must discover what qualities Lenin required of a true leader: these are to be found in his notes on the Gosplan. On December 27, 28 and 29 Lenin enumerates and repeats with great emphasis the qualities which, in his opinion, were appropriate to the head of one of the great institutions of the state—and therefore, by implication, to the state's chief leaders. The holder of such a post should have a sound scientific training in one of the branches of economics or technology; he must be capable of grasping "the totality of a situation"; he must possess a certain personal appeal to enable him to guide and supervise the work of those under him. At the same time, he must be an efficient organizer and administrator. But "the combination of these two kinds of qualities in one person will rarely be found, and it is hardly necessary."[6] In the case of an institution like the Gosplan, the administrative side is of secondary importance. Of the two men who would make an ideal combination, it is the scientific man who is also endowed with powers of reflection and an ability to get on with people who should be the leader. Lenin may well have believed that he had found in this formula an ideal situation for the direction of the state as a whole. He would hardly have labored the point to such an extent if it had merely been a question of keeping Krzhi-

[6] *Ibid.*, p. 351.

zhanovsky at the head of the Gosplan and making Pyatakov
his deputy. But Trotsky and Stalin did not form such a combination. They tended to exclude rather than complement
each other.

It was no doubt unfair to reproach Trotsky with an attitude
adopted in the circumstances of the civil war that at the
time was a perfectly plausible one and that proved entirely
successful. In different circumstances Trotsky was more
capable of approaching the problems of the state and of revolution in a scientific manner than the other members of the
Central Committee. He was perfectly capable of grasping
"the totality of a situation," as Lenin required of an ideal
leader. On the other hand, it was doubtful whether he possessed enough "personal appeal," and in any case Lenin knew
very well that he lacked certain of the qualities of a politician
in the narrow sense of the term: flexibility in his dealings with
others, a taste for tactics, a gift for maneuver and an ability
to steep himself uninhibitedly and unscrupulously in the
political mire of dictatorship. Later events showed that
Trotsky was incapable of playing such a game, let alone
winning it. Lenin was right to doubt his political abilities,
even though the criticisms made against him were not very
explicit. In short, Trotsky emerges from the considerations of
the "Testament" in a somewhat diminished position, mainly
because he is not placed above Stalin and because his former
non-Bolshevism, even though it cannot be held against him
personally, is nonetheless mentioned.

Though Lenin apparently finds nothing very definite to
reproach Stalin with, he does express one reservation: will he
show enough caution in the exercise of the immense power
concentrated in his hands? But however accurate the intuition that inspired this reservation, it had little political importance at the beginning of 1923 and could do nothing to

damage Stalin's position. If the notes had stopped at this point and then been read out at a Party Congress, they would have appeared to the delegates to be mainly concerned with maintaining a proper balance within the leadership and avoiding a split. In fact, it is perfectly obvious that the equitable distribution of praise and blame in the document was fully intended. Lenin was in no position to bequeath his power; he was not a monarch. He did not feel authorized to propose a successor to the Party, though the problem of the succession had preoccupied him even before his illness. As he awaited the moment "to quit the ranks," he tried not to affect the cohesion of his party by too marked a personal preference. And at the time of dictating these first notes, he may not yet have had one. Even if his preference already tended towards Trotsky, he had to conceal it so as not to poison relations between the leaders. He could not ignore the attitude towards Trotsky of fellow Bolsheviks such as Zinoviev and Kamenev, or of Stalin and various groups of Party militants. Trotsky's non-Bolshevism had already gone against him in a number of disputes in which Lenin had had to exert his own prestige to defend him. Lenin could not dream of imposing him as heir, especially in view of the fact that, until he had formed a new opinion of Stalin, he had not envisaged the possibility of having a single heir.

At this stage, in sum, Lenin suggested that the two most prominent leaders, Stalin and Trotsky, should preserve their pre-eminence; that Zinoviev and Kamenev should remain in second position, since the weakness they had shown at a time of great trial was not fortuitous and could therefore be repeated; and that the two youngest, Bukharin and Pyatakov, should remain in third position until such time as they matured. But since no better arrangement could be made, the Party must keep a careful watch on its leaders, as they were not free from faults and their rivalries might have fatal consequences. A proper watch should also be kept on the way in which Stalin used his power. In order to exercise such controls, the authority and prestige of the Central Committee must be strengthened. Lenin's percipience is apparent in the way in which, even at this stage, he notes the "detail" that was to upset the balance he was striving to maintain—the "unlimited authority" that made Stalin's position so much stronger than that of the other five. For the moment, he did not comment on this "detail," but he was later to elaborate its possible consequences when, after long reflection on fundamental questions, he returned to the problem of personalities.

In fact, since the state of Lenin's health continued unchanged, he went on working. Ten days after dictating the first notes, during which time his attention had been directed towards other problems, he added on January 4, 1923, a final section to his "Testament" that completely overthrew the delicate balance of the earlier entries, or rather corrected the real imbalance of which he was implicitly aware. Lenin proposed to deprive Stalin of his powers as General Secretary.

"Stalin is too rude, and this defect, though quite tolerable in our midst and in dealings among us Communists, becomes intolerable in a General Secretary. That is why I suggest that the comrades think about a way to remove Stalin from that post and appoint in his place another man who in all respects differs from Comrade Stalin in his superiority, that is, more tolerant, more loyal, more courteous and more considerate of the comrades, less capricious, etc."[7]

It might be thought that these words were the expression of a sudden reaction to some irritating event—and it would

[7] *Soch.,* Vol. XLV, p. 346.

be tempting to cite Stalin's offensive treatment of Krupskaya on December 22. Stalin would not have acted as he did if he had not known that the lion was mortally wounded, and Lenin, as he said in a letter written to Stalin two months later, was not the man to forgive such behavior: "I have no intention of forgetting so easily what has been done against me, and it goes without saying that what has been done against my wife I regard as having been done against me."[8] In fact, Krupskaya did not at the time tell Lenin of the affair for fear of the serious effect it might have on his health. She relieved her immediate indignation by complaining bitterly to Kamenev in a letter (reproduced in Appendix V). But it is quite possible that some days later she told her husband what had happened, either spontaneously or because, having noticed that something was amiss, he had plied her with questions. In his first burst of anger Lenin may then have dictated this note, in which he spoke only of Stalin's defects of character and made no criticisms of a political nature. The editors of the *Works* assume that Krupskaya did not tell Lenin of the event until the beginning of March. But this version is no more certain than any other. Moreover, we know enough about Lenin to look for an explanation more in keeping with his character as a leader for whom politics outweighed all other considerations. The first note of the "Testament" shows very clearly what Lenin's most urgent preoccupation was, and this is confirmed by a number of other facts. It would be futile to suppose that a personal affront to his wife—we must not forget that he considers such behavior "quite tolerable" in relations between Communists—could have driven him to a political action of a kind to upset the

[8] *Soch.*, Vol. LIV, p. 337. This letter is reproduced in Chapter 7, page 101.

balance of power within the Central Committee. He had far
more serious reasons for doing so. Proof of this is to be
found in the notes on the national question and autonomization dictated on December 30 and 31. Keeping to his work
schedule, he tackled these questions one week after dictating
the first notes.

This text is one of the most important in the whole
"Testament" and probably the most significant in that it enables us to appreciate the gravity of the crisis through which
Lenin was passing at this time, his intellectual honesty and
political courage. It is even quite likely that his anxiety over
political questions helped to hasten the decline of his health.

The reflections on the national question begin with a self-
criticism: "I suppose I have been very remiss with respect to
the workers of Russia for not having intervened energetically
and decisively enough on the notorious question of autonomization which, it appears, is officially called the question
of the Union of Soviet Socialist Republics."[9] There follows a
long personal justification, mainly on the grounds of his illness, then a description of the revealing effect produced by
Dzerzhinsky's report—Ordzhonikidze had lost his temper to
such an extent that he had struck an opposing Communist!
"What a mess we've got ourselves into!" Knowing Russia,
with its bureaucracy "hardly affected by the Soviet spirit,"
knowing above all the character of "that really Russian man,
the Great Russian chauvinist, in substance a rascal and a
tyrant, such as the typical Russian bureaucrat is," Lenin was
capable of realizing that his regime had not done enough to
defend the minority nations against the invasion of the Russian *dzerzhimordy,* or bullies. But the criticism went further:
the guilty were to be found not only, as he had previously

thought, among former members of the old oppressive bureaucracy; the Soviet regime itself, even the most highly
placed Party leaders, had behaved in a truly imperialist
fashion, if only in matters of detail. Lenin knew perfectly
well, and he was not afraid to say so, that such a situation
made nonsense of "all the sincerity of principle, all the defense of the principle of the struggle against imperialism"
proclaimed by the Party. This was all the more serious in
that "the morrow of world history will be a day when the
awakening peoples oppressed by imperialism are fully
aroused and the decisive long and hard struggle for their
liberation begins." There is no point in adding that the
Party's socialist, revolutionary sincerity was all the more
suspect when one considers the actions that Lenin was con-
tinually attacking.

According to Lenin, the Party leaders had not even understood the first principle that should guide them in seeking, in
an internationalist spirit, a solution to the national question.
The proletariat must, in its own interests, win the confidence
of the borderlands, which were profoundly mistrustful of the
majority nation that had subjected them to so many insults
and repeated acts of injustice. The situation was such that
if the larger nation was content simply to proclaim a formal
equality, its attitude could be described as bourgeois. In
order to make amends for the wrongs committed against the
small nations, the big nation must accept an inequality
unfavorable to itself. It must practice a kind of discrimination
against itself in order to compensate for the *de facto* inequality that continued to exist to the detriment of the small
nations. There must be an increase in the concessions made
to the small nations and in measures taken in their interest.
This was not the policy of Stalin, Ordzhonikidze and Dzerzhinsky. Lenin's condemnation is so severe that his deep

political hostility to them and their like can no longer be doubted. Stalin is accused of being in a violent hurry and of giving vent to dangerous expressions of anger against the so-called "social nationalists." Dzerzhinsky has revealed that "truly Russian" attitude so typical of Russianized expatriates from the borderlands. When placed in charge of a commission of inquiry he displayed such an unpardonable partiality that the work of his commission must be regarded as useless. The whole inquiry must be started again in order "to correct the enormous mass of errors and biased judgments which it undoubtedly contains." Lenin roundly accuses Ordzhonikidze and Stalin of acting like Great Russian bullies, of breaking the rules of proletarian internationalism and of falling into an imperialistic attitude. He demands an "exemplary punishment" for Ordzhonikidze—according to Trotsky, this involved exclusion from the Party, at least temporarily—and also an official condemnation of Stalin and Dzerzhinsky in view of their political responsibility for the affair. Moreover, he accuses them in turn of being "deviationists."[10] He recognizes that any project for autonomization "was probably essentially unjust and premature." He agrees that the Union should be maintained, but only on condition that the process of integration may be reversed if need be and the Union operate only in the spheres of foreign policy and defense, while in all other spheres "the complete independence of the old commissariats must be restored." In other words, there was to be a return to the relations that had previously existed, as from the next Congress of the Soviets. It is reasonable to believe, as does Professor Pipes, that if Lenin had not been finally incapacitated in March, "the final

[10] See below, Chapter 7.

structure of the Soviet Union would have been quite different from that which Stalin ultimately gave it."[11]

A similar hypothesis may be offered concerning the whole structure of the Soviet regime. As it is, Lenin dictated these reflections on autonomization just as the Congress that ratified the solution he had so criticized was opening. Fotieva affirms that this was no coincidence, for Lenin "was increasingly anxious about a correct solution of the national question."[12] The criticism of Stalin's national policy and of his treatment of the Georgians is sufficient explanation of Lenin's change of mind and of his eventual decision that Stalin should be deprived of his post. Lenin's mind was made up. From now on only tactical considerations would guide him in his choice of methods and timing for the defense of his new ideas.

[11] Pipes, *Formation of the Soviet Union*, p. 276.
[12] Fotieva, *Iz Vospominaniy*, p. 50.

7

"THE CLANDESTINE AFFAIR"

The first two months of 1923 were for Lenin a period of intense intellectual activity and of abrupt changes in his health. Sometimes he was in excellent humor and his doctors noted a marked improvement in his general condition. He was pleased with his dictations and joked with those around him. His doctors then allowed him additional periods for work and reading. Later, when he began to gain control once more of his right hand, he was even allowed to read the newspapers and receive visits. Lenin sometimes felt so well that one day he thought his illness was merely nervous in origin.[1] But these good moments alternated with others when he was extremely tired and suffered from loss of memory, difficulty with speaking, nervous tension and physical pain. Those around Lenin were very attentive to the ups and downs of his illness, and the members of the Political Bureau took careful note of them. During these two months, the future of the state and the fate of its leaders were in the balance; everything depended on whether Lenin would recover sufficiently to take part in the next Party Congress, and if so, what he would say.

Throughout January and February, in five articles developing the ideas expressed in the notes, Lenin worked out a vast program of political strategy for the Party Congress that was to be held a few weeks later. He was driven to hasten the completion of this work by the fear that he might not be able to attend the Congress and by the urgent nature of the reforms envisaged.

In the practical field, three questions in particular preoccupied him.

First, he wanted to know the findings of the census of civil servants in the large cities that had been carried out at his instigation. He was so suspicious of the bureaucracy that he made repeated requests to see what the results had been. In the end, his secretary was forced to admit that he would not be allowed to see the documents without Stalin's permission. Lenin had not known about this. According to Fotieva in her memoirs,[2] the affair provoked Lenin to an outburst of bad temper three days later, on January 10, and a month later, on February 12, caused an emotional crisis. One of his

---

[1] See the "Journal," February 14. We do not know what the doctors' diagnosis was at this time or how much Lenin knew about it. His death was later officially attributed to arteriosclerosis.

[2] Fotieva, *Iz Vospominaniy*, p. 70.

doctors, Förster, who was about to allow him newspapers and visits, suddenly put an end to his hopes and forbade "political information." When Lenin asked what he meant by the term, the doctor replied, "Well, for example, you were very interested in the question of the census of Soviet civil servants." This reply came as such a shock to Lenin that his lips trembled: the fact that the doctors should be so well informed about such details and capable of making such distinctions confirmed his worst suspicions. Fotieva notes prudently in the "Journal": "It is probable, moreover, that Lenin got the impression that it was not the doctors who gave the orders to the CC, but the CC to the doctors." In fact, for Fotieva, it was no longer a question of mere probability but of certainty.[3]

The second subject that preoccupied Lenin was his plan to merge the Commissariat of Workers' and Peasants' Inspection with the Central Control Commission. This was to be the keystone of his larger plans to reorganize the Central Committee and the whole summit of the Party structure. We see from the "Journal" that he was constantly seeking the advice of his deputy Tsyurupa and of the members of the commissariat, to whom these plans were communicated. He urged them to act, to pave the way for these important changes in the state. In the end, he decided to bring up the whole question before the Party Congress.

But the subjects that took up most of his time—and concerned him most—were the Georgian affair and the constitution of the USSR. Lenin had already expressed his opinion on the principle involved and passed judgment on the individuals concerned in his memorandum of the end of December. In view of the exceptional measures that were to be

[3] See Fotieva's notes in the "Journal" for February 1 and 3.

taken against those responsible, he had to act, and act quickly, if he was to assemble, before the opening of the Congress, the detailed evidence required to support his allegations. By means of the "Journal" and various other writings scattered throughout the fifth edition of the *Works,* a fairly clear idea can be gained of Lenin's "great conspiracy." On January 24, after finishing and sending off to *Pravda* his article on the Workers' Inspection, Lenin called Fotieva and asked her for the documents of Dzerzhinsky's commission of inquiry in Georgia. He did not know that this question was about to be discussed at the Politburo. The next day he asked again whether Stalin or Dzerzhinsky had sent him the papers. Meanwhile, the Politburo approved the conclusions of the commission, condemned the Georgians once again, and whitewashed Ordzhonikidze and Stalin. The commission had suggested that Mdivani, Makharadze, Tsintsadze and a number of others should be recalled to Moscow. This too was approved, and Professor Pipes claims that the order was sent out even before the bureau had met.[4]

Fotieva managed to keep abreast of all that was happening at the top. Moreover, on February 3 she found an opportunity of letting Lenin know too, as if "by clumsiness." When she asked once again for the papers to be sent to Lenin, she came up against strong opposition. Dzerzhinsky referred Fotieva to Stalin, but Stalin was not in Moscow. In the end, Stalin informed her that he could not give her the papers until the bureau had given its permission. Lenin's request disturbed him. He asked Fotieva whether perhaps she did not let Lenin know too much in view of the decision that all information about day-to-day matters should be withheld from him. Obviously, Fotieva denied this, but she repeated what

---

[4] Pipes, *Formation,* p. 282, and Fotieva, *Iz Vospominaniy,* p. 54.

had been said to Lenin, who remarked acidly, "So the national affair is a day-to-day matter, is it?" Lenin had insisted too strenuously for Stalin to be able to refuse him the papers without being covered by the bureau, for of course, the national question was not a day-to-day matter. Without supplying further details as to her sources, Fotieva reports an exchange of messages between Kamenev and Stalin during a meeting of the bureau:

Kamenev: "Since Vladimir Ilich insists, I think it would be even worse to refuse."

Stalin: "I don't know. Let him do as he likes."

But this was obviously not what he wanted, for he demanded to be freed from his responsibility for Lenin's medical supervision. This request was not granted and the bureau gave its permission for Lenin to see the papers, without really knowing what he intended to do with them.[5]

Lenin merely wanted to check the facts for himself. With this aim in view, he formed a private commission of inquiry composed of Gorbunov, his assistant-secretary at the Sovnarkom, and two of his secretaries, Fotieva and Gliasser. The first questions that this commission was to clear up—others were to follow as the study of the papers progressed—were the following:

"1) Why was the former Georgian CC accused of deviationism?

"2) Why were they accused of breaking Party discipline?

"3) Why was the Zakkraykom accused of repressing the Georgian CC?

"4) Physical means of oppression (the 'biomechanics').

"5) The line adopted by the CC of the RCP in the absence and in the presence of Vladimir Ilich.

---

[5] Fotieva, *Iz Vospominaniy*, pp. 64–65.

"6) With whom did the commission come into contact in the course of its work? Did it inquire only into the accusations made against the Georgian CC, or also into those made against the Zakkraykom? Did it study the affair of the 'biomechanics'?

"7) The present situation: the electoral campaign, the Mensheviks, oppression, the national quarrel."[6]

Armed with these instructions and urged on constantly by Lenin, the three secretaries set to work and hoped to arrive at their conclusions within three weeks. Lenin pressed Fotieva with ever more detailed questions, for his fears seemed increasingly well founded and the responsibility of the individuals implicated more serious. On February 14, additional instructions were given to the commission that reveal a good deal about Lenin's state of mind and his determination to leave no stone unturned:

"Three elements: (1) it is not permitted to strike someone; (2) concessions are indispensable; (3) one cannot compare a small state with a large one.

"Did Stalin know (of the incident)? Why didn't he do something about it?"

The personal error has become a political error of the utmost gravity. Further on we read: "The label 'deviationists' for chauvinistic deviation and Menshevism indicates the same deviation among the *velikoderzhavniki*." This term, which Lenin was to use increasingly to describe the men he was criticizing, is difficult to translate; it suggests the idea of chauvinism, of Great Power egocentricity, of imperialism. Lenin was now determined to eliminate this adverse tendency

---

[6] *Soch.*, Vol. XLV, pp. 606–7. The "biomechanics" is the blow given to Kabanidze by Ordzhonikidze.

in the Party. In a sense he moved into action immediately, for he gave the following order:

"Directive from Vladimir Ilich: refer in Soltz's presence to the idea that he (Vladimir Ilich) is on the side of the weaker. Suggest to one of the offended parties that he is on their side."[7]

Lenin, then, no longer wished either to keep his thoughts secret or to remain neutral; on the contrary, he tried to warn those most concerned. When Soltz learned this he no doubt told certain members of the Political Bureau and probably Stalin. The Georgians too must have conveyed the news to one of their protectors. It must have circulated, then, though in a restricted way at first, sufficient to increase vigilance on both sides. Documents that were too compromising disappeared from the dossier. To her astonishment, Fotieva learned from Soltz that "Comrades of the Georgian CC provided him with evidence of all kinds of vexations against the Georgians (supporters of the former CC of the CPG). Concerning the incident—the offensive treatment of Kabanidze by Ordzhonikidze—the Central Control Commission was in possession of a declaration from the victim, but it has disappeared. When I asked, 'What do you mean, disappeared?' Comrade Soltz replied, 'Just disappeared.' But it doesn't make much difference because the CCC has an objective account by Rykov, who was present at the time."[8] (Without going into too much detail, one might well question Rykov's objectivity. On December 9, 1922, when he submitted his report to Lenin, he had not breathed a word about the incident. Lenin learned of it only three days later, from Dzerzhinsky himself.)

---

[7] *Ibid.*, p. 107. These notes were taken by Fotieva. Soltz was one of the leaders of the Central Control Commission.

[8] Fotieva, *Iz Vospominaniy*, p. 75.

Lenin spurred on the work of his commission; his health was precarious and he wanted at all costs to deliver a memorandum on the national question to the coming Congress. New information might necessitate an extension of the inquiry, perhaps even sending someone to the scene of the incident, all of which would take a great deal of time. Any delay in the commission's work, he told Fotieva on February 14, might ruin its chances of success, and that would be a great blow to him. There are no notes in the "Journal" from February 14 to March 5. Moreover, the editors of the *Works* provide no information about these three weeks. Lenin may well have written nothing during this period, and in any case, the secretaries were very busy on their work for the "clandestine commission."[9] One thing is known, however: on March 3 the commission presented its conclusions.[10] But the document has not yet come to light. Why has the Institute of Marxism-Leninism not yet made it public? Could it have "disappeared," like Kabanidze's complaint? For the present, nothing is known about it. In any case, the results of the commission's work must have given the last two active days of Lenin's life the character of a major struggle. They must have made Lenin more bitter and more angry with his colleagues than ever and strengthened his conviction that the sorry Georgian affair was merely one symptom of a much deeper sickness. But Lenin's declining health did not allow him to live much longer in such a state of emotional and nervous tension. His illness grew rapidly more serious, and owing to a combination of his disturbed emotional state and

[9] However, Fotieva mentions in *Iz Vospominaniy* some notes taken down on January 10 (p. 70) and February 16 (p. 75). But they do not appear in the "Journal."

[10] *Soch.*, Vol. XLV, p. 714.

the steady increase of the sclerosis, he began to feel very ill.[11]

This was no doubt the reason that drove him, without further delay, to deliver the blows that he had been preparing against his opponents for the past two months, even if it was still a little early to do so. The first three attacks were directed against a single objective: Stalin. Lenin managed to conceal from his doctors the deep emotional stress that he felt when he took these decisions, and told them, Fotieva reports, that he was merely dictating a few business letters. About noon on March 5, he called for Volodicheva and dictated two letters.

The first, which was strictly secret and written in an unusually affectionate tone, was addressed to Trotsky and was to be read out to him at once over the telephone. Here it is:

"I earnestly ask you to undertake the defense of the Georgian affair at the Central Committee of the Party. That affair is now under 'persecution' at the hands of Stalin and Dzerzhinsky and I cannot rely on their impartiality. Indeed, quite the contrary! If you would agree to undertake its defense, I could be at rest. If for some reason you do not agree, send me back all the papers. I will consider that a sign of your disagreement.

With the very best comradely greetings,

LENIN"[12]

Lenin could do nothing without an ally. Trotsky was not only the sole possible ally, he could also be depended on. With the protection of Lenin alive, Trotsky was still unbeatable in the early months of 1923. The form of closing

---

[11] See the "Journal" for March 5 and 6, and Trotsky, *The Stalin School of Falsification*, p. 71.

[12] *Soch.*, Vol. LIV, p. 329.

used by Lenin to Trotsky was so warm that Stalin, when forced to read out the letter before the Central Committee in July 1926—by which time his position could no longer be seriously threatened—preferred nonetheless to change it to a mere "With communist greetings."[13] This letter represented a great victory for Trotsky. It meant that the "pact against bureaucracy," which Lenin had proposed to him at the beginning of December and for which he had had to wait for so long, had at last been concluded.[14] It also meant that he could really feel that he had Lenin's support in the question of the succession and that he could feel reassured about the final outcome of the intrigue that had been directed against him since Lenin fell ill.

Lenin had taken the political decisions and could now allow himself to follow up the attack and settle a private score with Stalin. While awaiting Trotsky's reply to his first letter, he began to dictate another to Stalin concerning his insulting treatment of Krupskaya, but because he was tired, and also perhaps because he had doubts about its tactical wisdom, he decided to put off the writing of this difficult letter until the following day. Lenin was probably wondering whether such a personal attack might not diminish the criticism of principle and whether it was in line with his general plan of action. But the next day, when he had Trotsky's reply, which was undoubtedly in the affirmative,[15] he completed the dictation of the letter, reread the whole correspondence, and asked Volodicheva to take the letter to Stalin and await his reply. Here is the text of the message; it is obvious that it was intended to hit at Stalin as hard as possible:

[13] Trotsky, *Stalin School of Falsification*, p. 71.
[14] *Ibid.*, p. 73.
[15] See the note on Trotsky's reply in Appendix VIII.

"To Comrade Stalin,
highly secret, personal,
copies to Comrades Kamenev and Zinoviev

Very respectable Comrade Stalin,

You allowed yourself to be so ill-mannered as to call my wife on the telephone and to abuse her. She has agreed to forget what was said. Nevertheless, she has told Zinoviev and Kamenev about the incident. I have no intention of forgetting what has been done against me, and it goes without saying that what was done against my wife I also consider to have been directed against myself. Consequently, I must ask you to consider whether you would be inclined to withdraw what you said and to apologize, or whether you prefer to break off relations between us.

Respectfully yours,
LENIN"[16]

As that day, March 6, wore on, Lenin felt worse and worse. But he was determined to press on. The day before, Fotieva and Gliasser, who acted as go-betweens for Lenin and Trotsky (who was himself confined to another apartment in the Kremlin with lumbago), had told Trotsky that Kamenev was leaving for the Caucasus and that he could, if he so wished, entrust him with any business he might have there.[17] We do not know exactly what the purpose of Kamenev's visit was. But Trotsky, who had received the memorandum of December 30 and other papers by Lenin on Georgia, suggested that they should be shown to Kamenev so that he might begin to take certain measures on the spot. Fotieva

---

[16] *Soch.*, Vol. LIV, pp. 329–30.
[17] *Ibid.*, p. 329.

went off to ask Lenin and came back to Trotsky with a categorical negative: "It is entirely out of the question. Vladimir Ilich says that Kamenev would show the letters to Stalin and Stalin would make a rotten compromise in order then to deceive."[18] This probably took place in the morning. Shortly after the first reply, Fotieva returned to Trotsky with new instructions from Lenin and a copy of another letter. Lenin now proposed to divulge everything to Kamenev, and even to let him see the brief note addressed to the so-called Georgian deviationists:

"(*strictly secret*)
To Comrades Mdivani, Makharadze and others:
(*copy to Comrades Trotsky and Kamenev*)

Esteemed Comrades:

I follow your affair with all my heart. I am outraged at the rudeness of Ordzhonikidze and the connivance of Stalin and Dzerzhinsky. I am preparing for you notes and a speech.

> With esteem,
> LENIN

March 6, 1923."[19]

This was very different from the irritated reply he had sent to the Georgians on October 21. Lenin had arrived at diametrically opposite conclusions. He did not hide the fact: on the contrary, it was all the more reason to defend the Georgians now.

---

[18] Trotsky, *Stalin School of Falsification*, p. 71. We can confirm Trotsky's account in general terms by reference to the "Journal" and our other sources. Although he sometimes makes an error of twenty-four hours in his chronology of events, we may take him as a reliable witness in this case.

[19] *Soch.*, Vol. LIV, p. 330.

Trotsky, astonished by Lenin's sudden change of mind, demanded an explanation. Fotieva said that she supposed that "it is probably because Vladimir Ilich is getting worse and is in a hurry to do what he can." There is every reason to believe Trotsky when he says that one of Lenin's secretaries, probably Gliasser, told him that Vladimir Ilich was preparing a "bomb" against Stalin.[20]

Despite Lenin's clearly expressed desire that the letter demanding an apology should be taken to Stalin, Krupskaya tried to prevent its being sent. Quite obviously, she was already afraid of the Gensek even at this stage. She asked the secretaries to delay sending the letter. But the following day Volodicheva refused to equivocate any longer: it was her job to carry out Lenin's orders. Krupskaya sought advice before making up her mind and, as so often, it was to the amiable Kamenev that she turned. This was how he learned that Vladimir Ilich was planning "to crush Stalin politically."[21] Volodicheva then took the letter to Stalin, who replied on the spot with apologies. This was later revealed by Lenin's sister. But Lenin knew nothing of these apologies. That day, March 7, he suffered another serious attack. On March 10, half his body was paralyzed. He never recovered the power of speech.[22]

Lenin's political life was now over. He was only fifty-three years old. He died eleven months later on January 21, 1924. His iron constitution continued the hopeless struggle right to the end.

---

[20] Trotsky, *Stalin School of Falsification*, p. 75.

[21] Deutscher, *The Prophet Unarmed*, p. 90.

[22] See Appendix X, which concerns the course of Lenin's illness after the relapse of March 10.

8

RUSSIA
BETWEEN
WEST AND
EAST

The most characteristic and most striking part of Lenin's thought, during the last eighty days that he was still capable of forming and communicating it, concerned his judgments of individuals. But these judgments were, in a sense, only indicative. For Lenin, they were always related to the general problems that his state had to face.

The major problem, of course, concerned the world political situation. An analysis of this situation was an indispensable prerequisite for any correct assessment of all other problems. Without it, there could be no understanding of

the broad lines of historical development, no substance behind the leaders' hopes or fears for the future. But the world
situation was now developing in a very different way from
that expected by the Bolsheviks after their seizure of power.
No revolution had taken place in Western Europe. The only
country where a revolution had very nearly taken place—
Germany—had been crushed by the Allies. The victorious
nations, on the other hand, had acquired an unexpected
stability and seemed to be in a position to offer their prole-
tariats enough advantages to make the possibilities of revolution in the West recede for the moment. Realizing that Russia
was now alone in Europe, Lenin began to look elsewhere for
support, and it was to the East that he turned with ever
growing confidence.

In Asia, he saw the beginnings of a process of immense
potentiality. The Asian masses, oppressed by the same forces
that had subjugated Germany, were entering a capitalist
period. But at the same time, they were undergoing a period
of revolutionary unrest of a nationalist and anti-imperialist
kind. It was rather in this direction that Lenin foresaw an
end, in the long run, to Russian isolation and a hope for a
revival of the revolutionary forces in the world:

"In the last analysis, the outcome of the struggle will be
determined by the fact that Russia, India, China, etc., account for the overwhelming majority of the population of
the globe. And during the past few years it is this majority
that has been drawn into the struggle for emancipation with
extraordinary rapidity, so that in this respect there cannot be
the slightest doubt what the final outcome of the world
struggle will be."[1]

Although the final outcome is still uncertain today, the

[1] *Soch.*, Vol. XLV, p. 404. See Appendix IX.

prediction of the underlying movement of contemporary history is accurate enough. With his profound grasp of reality, Lenin also foresaw that the future development of the revolutionary process would take forms that were still more specific and more disturbing, for overschematic Marxists, than those it had known in Russia. It was in this context that Lenin questioned the specificity of the Russian Revolution. He explained it in terms of Russia's position between the world of capitalist civilization and that of the Asiatic East, with a preponderance at the time of writing of Eastern elements. An explanation of the Stalinist phenomenon has sometimes been sought in terms of an Oriental heritage: this interpretation is quite Leninist. It is not without interest in this matter to quote a passage from the article "Our Revolution," written against the theses of the Social Democrats. Lenin criticized these theses for not taking into account that because "Russia stands on the borderline between the civilized countries and the countries which this war has for the first time definitely brought into the orbit of civilization—all the Oriental, non-European countries—she could and was, indeed, bound to reveal certain distinguishing features; although these, of course, are in keeping with the general line of world development, they distinguish her revolution from those which took place in the West European countries and introduce certain partial innovations as the revolution moves on to the countries of the East."[2]

Lenin sees this as a source of difficulty and weakness. For a quarter of a century following his death it was to lead Russia into a system that some commentators have described as an "Asiatic mode of production." Yet at the same time it was also, from a strategic point of view, almost an advantage:

[2] *Ibid.*, p. 379.

the Western side of Russia was too weak to trigger off revolutions in the West, but her Asiatic side seemed to have a better chance of acting as an accelerator and a model for the millions in the East. Lenin was convinced of eventual victory in this direction, but he knew that it would be in the distant future. The problem of the statesman was to discover means whereby Russia could hold out until the arrival of these reinforcements. Lenin did not hide from his fellow countrymen —it must be remembered that his declarations were published in the press—that they were still a long way from victory. Would Russia continue to benefit from the conflicts between the West and Japan that had operated in her favor at the time of the civil war? Lenin refused to affirm that she would. He did not hesitate to make optimistic prophecies about the wisdom of history in general, but he prudently refrained from making forecasts that were too reassuring for the immediate future.

It will be noticed that Lenin's approach in this matter was not the one adopted by his successors under the slogan "socialism in one country." On the contrary, for Lenin it was a question of *proderzhatsiya,* of holding out until reinforcements arrived and, in the meantime, of building not socialism at once, but a society of transition. In "Better Fewer, But Better," he declares: "We, too, lack enough civilization to enable us to pass straight on to socialism." The main idea in this article, which contains the essence of the legacy he was so anxious to leave his people before he died, was that their aims should be more modest, more realistic and less ambitious; they must beware of megalomania. But this realism had not yet succeeded in dissipating the deep malaise that the specific situation of the Russian Revolution had aroused in its most devoted adherents. It seemed paradoxical, not to say aberrational, that proletarian power should be incapable of carrying out the tasks for which it had been created. Although Lenin was mainly concerned with assuring the practical survival of the Revolution, he too was affected by this malaise and consequently did his utmost to legitimize the Revolution in terms of Marxist theory. Because the Marxists were convinced that they were able to predict, more accurately than anyone else, the course of historical development, it was embarrassing for them that what was actually happening did not correspond to certain ready-made concepts.

Indeed, the Russian Revolution fitted in so badly with the generally accepted interpretation of Marxism that it appeared to its adversaries as nothing short of "anti-Marxist." The Mensheviks, beaten and condemned in the arena of historical action, largely by Lenin's political genius, were now in a position to avenge themselves, if only on a theoretical plane. The seizure of political power in the absence of an adequate infrastructure, the dictatorship of the proletariat almost without a proletariat, led by a party in which the proletariat was in the minority, the readmission of capitalism after a supposedly socialist revolution, almost unlimited power being invested in an enormous bureaucratic state machine—all these undeniable facts were in flagrant contradiction to both Marxist theory and common sense. And now Lenin was pinning his hopes on the precapitalist masses of the East, instead of on the civilized West! On his sickbed, Lenin studied these criticisms. The reply of the theoretician was no more orthodox than the action of the statesman:

"What if the complete hopelessness of the situation, by stimulating the efforts of the workers and peasants tenfold, offered us the opportunity to create the fundamental requisites of civilization in a different way from that of the West European countries? . . .

"If a definite level of culture is required for the building of socialism . . . why cannot we begin by first achieving the prerequisites for that definite level of culture in a revolutionary way, and *then*, with the aid of the workers' and peasants' government and the Soviet system, proceed to overtake the other nations?"

Better still, Lenin adds, referring to a somewhat unexpected source: "Napoleon, I think, wrote: '*On s'engage . . . et puis on voit*'."[3] In fact the Soviet Union, followed by China and Cuba, has proved that it was possible to seize power first and attain the level of other nations later. Nevertheless, the maxim *On s'engage et puis on voit* is not entirely devoid of ambiguity. Lenin, who was so thoroughly Marxist in his *Weltanschauung* and in his understanding of social reality, who believed that action should always be based on an assessment of the strength of the social forces involved, to whom any spirit of adventurism was so alien, seemed to be saying nevertheless that the timing of the seizure of power and the manner in which it was seized could not be strictly calculated in terms of a theoretical historicosocial analysis. The revolutionary act, like all politics, is in a sense an art, in which realism is intimately linked with a taste for risk. No revolution is in complete accordance with the theory that preceded it and was used in achieving it. This was why Lenin's message to future revolutionaries—though it seemed close to a call to adventure—emphasized above all that they must be capable of rejecting outworn dogmas, however useful these may have been in the past. In this sense, it contained

[3] *Ibid.*, pp. 380–81.

an implicit warning against dogmas that might be made out of Lenin's own theories.

All this did not come very easily to Lenin; and he would not have felt this curious need to justify his victory if he had felt assured as to the survival of his regime. But this was not the case. The Revolution might still be crushed, and Lenin did not know how history would then judge it.

But the list of dangers that faced the Soviet state was not confined to international problems. The new regime had to maneuver in increasingly complicated circumstances.[4] Since it had been decided to hold out as long as necessary, what program, what internal reforms were needed?

Lenin was certainly concerned about the tumor of bureaucracy, but in his opinion the gravest threat did not lie in that direction. A split between the workers and the peasants would, he believed, mean the end of the Revolution. The analysis of postrevolutionary Russian society, which had generally been based on the existence of two essential classes, now, with the introduction of the NEP, had to integrate a third, the bourgeoisie. The future looked gloomier than ever. By offering it a possible ally, one increased the chance of the peasantry defecting. The alternative was as follows: "in the final analysis, the fate of our Republic will depend on whether the peasant masses will stand by the working class, loyal to their alliance, or whether they will permit the 'Nepmen,' i.e. the new bourgeoisie, to drive a wedge between them and the working class, to split them off from the working class."[5] The alliance on which the existence of the regime depended was a precarious one—Lenin did not hide the fact. It was true that for the moment the small and the very small

4 *Ibid.*, pp. 343–44.
5 *Ibid.*, pp. 387–88.

peasantry, born of the Revolution, had faith in the Soviet system: "But with this faith and it alone it is not easy for us to keep going until the socialist revolution is victorious in more developed countries."[6] And the peasantry was too backward for its support to be taken for granted, especially as the civil war and foreign intervention had weakened the country's economy.

Such a social basis compromised the stability of both the state and the Party—that of the Party being already threatened by the possibility of a split among the leaders. Here too Lenin felt the need to justify by reference to Marxist theory his views on the importance of the relations between individuals in historical development—an importance that had been considerably minimized in the sociological writings of Plekhanov, the father of Russian Marxism. Here too, it was Lenin who was proved right.

Lenin had to face a double danger: from the alliance of workers and peasants on the one hand and from a possible split within the Party on the other. The first demanded certain long-term measures and the second an immediate reorganization of the upper echelons of the government machine. In this context, Lenin's plans must be regarded as emergency measures, even if most of them would take some time to bear fruit. Moreover, the two sets of remedies were closely linked, since the highest possible cost-effectiveness of the government machine would help to win the support of the peasants. The peasant must certainly be won over, but not by direct communist propaganda. Lenin warns the Party against such an undertaking:

"Under no circumstances must this be understood to mean that we should immediately propagate purely and strictly

[6] *Ibid.,* p. 401.

communist ideas in the countryside. As long as our country-side lacks the material basis for communism, it will be, I should say, harmful, in fact, I should say, fatal for communism to do so."[7]

Lenin was thinking of a system of initiation by which workers' cells from the town would spread their urban, Soviet influence in the countryside, on condition of course—for Lenin knew his world—that these activities remained entirely voluntary and were prevented from turning into bureaucratic bodies like the other branches of the Party machine.

The whole of Lenin's program for the peasants might be summed up by the slogan "cultural revolution." This notion, now so fashionable in a country that claims to be Leninist, was understood by Lenin himself in what can only be described as a passionately realistic and antidogmatic sense. Lenin railed pitilessly against all those who talked so glibly of "proletarian culture" while in fact the masses lived in a state of "semi-Asiatic ignorance." It would be far better to try and acquire some culture as such, or even, more modestly, to learn to read and write. Before expatiating on proletarian culture, it was necessary to attain the level of an average Western country: "For a start, we should be satisfied with real bourgeois culture; for a start, we should be glad to dispense with the cruder types of prebourgeois culture, i.e., bureaucratic culture or serf culture, etc. In matters of culture, haste and sweeping measures are most harmful."[8] Although this program was called a "revolution," it would take a long historical period to be carried out. It was a long-term project: "The entire people must go through a period of cultural

[7] *Ibid.,* p. 367.
[8] *Ibid.,* p. 389.

development." In a sense, that was *all* Russia needed. "There are now no other devices needed to advance to socialism," Lenin said in his article "On Cooperation."

This task must be the regime's main concern. The figure of the people's schoolmaster must be given new prestige and certain material privileges (which at this time meant priority in the distribution of bread). This aspect of Lenin's program was among the more utopian of his grand design: in fact, the position of the village schoolmaster was to remain a rather unfavorable one for a long time to come.

Lenin's socioeconomic plan for the rural areas, his "cooperative plan," seems to have been closely linked with the "cultural revolution," and was all the more important for being so. But this too was a long-term project.

For Lenin the NEP was and should long remain the socioeconomic framework within which the peasant could operate, a system he could understand and which conformed to his own interests. Before his death, Lenin became convinced that this idea should be the guiding principle of a long period of transition, and that "all we actually need under NEP is to organize the population of Russia in cooperative societies on a sufficiently large scale."[9] The question now arises as to how much such an idea can be reconciled with the regime's socialist objectives. Lenin had always regarded the cooperative system as an essentially bourgeois mode of economic activity, so it might well be asked whether the capitalist tendencies of the NEP would not strengthen the supposedly bourgeois character of the peasant cooperative movement. Lenin performed a complete doctrinal *volte-face* on this subject. He now believed that cooperation was the right method of guiding the peasant class towards socialist structures. He

[9] *Ibid.*, p. 370.

believed this so firmly that cooperation came to occupy in
his plans the place left vacant by his reluctant abandonment
of state capitalism after its practical failure. Because the
state and the principal means of production were now in the
workers' hands, cooperation had ceased to be the essentially
bourgeois and mercantile institution it had formerly been. It
would be a socialist institution that would develop in step
with socialism. This cooperation would enable each peasant
to participate in the building of socialism by methods that
were familiar to him. The right path seemed to have been
found: "Strictly speaking, there is '*only*' one thing we have
left to do and that is to make our people so 'enlightened' that
they understand all the advantages of everybody participating in the work of the cooperatives, and to organize this
participation. '*Only*' that. There are now no other devices
needed to advance to socialism." What he meant was that
socialism could be attained only after the long period necessary for the realization of the initial objective. With his new
cooperative strategy in view, Lenin also redefined socialism
in general: "And given social ownership of the means of
production, given the class victory of the proletariat over
the bourgeoisie, the system of civilized cooperators is the
system of socialism."[10] Lenin did not have time to develop
this idea in his article, although his line of thought is perfectly
clear. The only rather confused passages are those in which
he tries to explain in what sense a cooperative (and we are
not told what kind of cooperative—whether for consump-
tion, sale or production) can be socialist, and just as socialist
as a state-owned enterprise—about whose socialist character
Lenin was in no doubt. This change of doctrine creates as
many problems as it solves. For example, Lenin is not speak-

[10] *Ibid.*, p. 373.

ing of production cooperatives; the functions of those he envisages would be mainly commercial. The Russian peasant and trader "run trade in an Asiatic manner, but to be a good trader one must trade in the European manner." Cooperation will enable the peasants to become "cultured traders." When this happens, says Lenin, Russia will have caught up with the advanced countries.

So, might it be argued, socialism is a regime of "cultured traders"? This was obviously not what Lenin meant. For him, the terms "socialism" and "communism" were so much a matter for the distant future that he did not hesitate to use them for their present mobilizing force and propaganda value, without much care for scientific accuracy in what, after all, were merely reflections on medium-term political strategy. The same article provides a key to the understanding of his rather cavalier way of treating such concepts. Defending himself for having abandoned the idea of state capitalism, against certain Communists who, showing more concern than he for doctrinal purity, had constantly criticized its use, Lenin remarks: "They did not notice that the practical purpose was always important to me." This explains why, in these articles, the most important tasks for the present were termed "socialist" or "communist," if he thought this would bring the state nearer to its ultimate objectives. Since he now believed that cooperation was absolutely necessary to the state, he was quite willing to provide it with enough respectability to win the serious attention of the upper echelons of the Party. Every social order, he explained, is born with the support of a particular class; it was useful to support the cooperative system by giving it capital and various other advantages. Such was his suggested plan of action, but his successors followed him only very partially in this sphere.

9
THE REFORM
OF THE
GOVERNMENTAL
STRUCTURES

Since it was inconceivable that socialism could be brought about in the present state of Russian society through spontaneous pressure from below, the Bolsheviks were left with only one way of achieving their desired aim: through their control of the state machine. It was hardly surprising therefore that the most fully developed theme in Lenin's writings at this time should be the reform of the governmental structures. For if this power was not used with the utmost prudence, it too might slip from their grasp. Ever since the end of the civil war, Lenin had constantly reiterated the injunction "Let us learn to govern."

In the struggle against all the undesirable tendencies in the state and Party machines, Lenin saw only one point of departure: the reorganization of the Communist elite and, above all, of the Party leadership. It was at the top that changes must be initiated and an example set for the rest of society. At the time even the big commissariats were functioning badly, and Lenin did not spare them his harshest criticism. But there was worse to come: he was concerned about the functioning of his own Sovnarkom, which explains why, throughout 1922, he devoted a considerable amount of the time that was still available to him to reorganizing the functions of his deputies and, through them, of the whole central government. He found to his horror that a hundred and twenty commissions had been set up by the Sovnarkom, whereas, in his opinion, sixteen would have been perfectly adequate to perform the same tasks.

On the other hand, on his return to work after a period of illness, Lenin realized that during his absence the two machines, the government and the Party, had ceased to work in harmony and were either duplicating each other's functions or merely "ticking over." The senior civil servants, even the commissars themselves, tended to evade responsibility, either by hiding behind the hundred and twenty commissions, or by submitting every question, however unimportant, even sometimes quite routine questions, to the Political Bureau.

The first and most important recommendation, which Lenin announced on December 23, was that the number of members of the Central Committee should be increased to one hundred. In this way, Lenin hoped to attenuate conflict between rival leaders, revive the rather tarnished prestige of the Central Committee, and entrust it with a new task: that of reconstructing the whole state apparatus on a new basis.[1]

Lenin does not explain why the prestige of the Central Committee needed to be revived; but it is easy to see how, when faced with the twenty other members of this body, the seven members of the Politburo enjoyed excessive influence. After the Eleventh Congress, these seven were Lenin, Stalin, Trotsky, Zinoviev, Kamenev, Tomsky and Rykov.[2] In the second version of his plan Lenin proposed to form, in addition to the enlarged Central Committee, a Central Control Commission of seventy-five to a hundred members in a large new body whose specific task would be the construction of the state apparatus. The original idea was that the new members should be recruited from among the workers, but this clause was finally abandoned on the grounds that the tasks assigned to them would be too complex to be properly carried out by factory workers alone.

The Central Committee and the new Central Control Commission would together form the new Central Committee, a large assembly of one hundred and fifty to two hundred members, which would constitute in fact a Party conference and meet six times a year. Moreover, the presidium of the Central Control Commission would take part in the work of the Politburo, in both an active and a supervisory capacity. It would make sure that the Central Committee and the bureau functioned correctly, checking all documents, and so forth, without consideration of persons, even the Gensek himself.

The Central Committee would not only be strengthened,

---

[1] Lenin returned to these ideas in his articles "On the Workers' and Peasants' Inspection" (the first version of which is reproduced in *Soch.*, Vol. XLV, pp. 442–50) and "Better Fewer, But Better," the latter reproduced in Appendix IX.

[2] And four deputies: Bukharin, Kuibyshev, Kalinin and Molotov.

therefore, but would be given wider responsibilities. One last problem remained: where would the expertise and method come from for the training of an effective body of civil servants? Lenin came back to the institution which he himself had created, but which had subsequently disappointed him so much: the Workers' and Peasants' Inspection, also known under its three Russian initials, RKI. Its function was the supervision of the work of the government organizations and other administrations. Under Stalin's direction—he was Commissar of the Inspection from March 1919 to April 25, 1922—it had become an overgrown, highly bureaucratic body, comprising some twelve thousand civil servants, very few of whom were workers. The *chinovniki* had succeeded very quickly in taking over the institutions that had been specially created to combat bureaucracy.

Trotsky had begun to attack the RKI at the beginning of 1922. At that time Lenin still defended the commissariat, and therefore indirectly its head, but in his last writings he depicted it as a haven of ineptitude, a "hopeless affair": "None of the commissariats is worse organized than the RKI, and it is utterly devoid of authority." These barbs, directed at Stalin through the commissariat for which he had been responsible, were probably the reason why the article "Better Fewer, But Better," which had been finished on February 10, did not appear in *Pravda* until March 4.[3]

The whole unwieldly mess must be tidied up as soon as possible; the commissariat should retain a staff of three or four hundred of the best specialists in the scientific study of

[3] According to Deutscher, *The Prophet Unarmed*, pp. 88–90, a majority of the bureau was against publication; Kuibyshev had even suggested printing a special copy of *Pravda,* for Lenin's use, that would contain the article in question. But Trotsky insisted that the article should be published in the normal way, and his suggestion was finally carried with the support of Kamenev or Zinoviev.

administration and work methods, recruited either from among former members of the RKI or elsewhere. In this way they could exercise an educative role among the new members of the Central Committee. Moreover, as far as governmental administration was concerned, the new RKI would merge with the Central Control Commission to form a sort of model commissariat representing "all that is best in our social order." The specialists of the RKI would enjoy a more privileged position, not only from a material point of view but also in terms of prestige, since they would be partly fused with the supreme power in the state.

The new Central Control Commission would also act, on occasion, as a sort of academy or institute; it would devote part of its time to the study, under the direction of experts, of management, control and the rationalization of work. This new CCC-RKI, with its five hundred experts and Control Commission members, would become an institution of an ability and efficiency unequaled in the state, a unique super-commissariat of organization and supervision, whose function would be to diffuse correct methods at every level of public administration.

To learn to govern and to teach the administrative machine to do so, to gain as a result the confidence of the peasants and to reduce to a minimum the risks of a break in the "alliance," to prevent the danger of an "accidental" split in the Party, to help the state to maneuver more freely on the international scene: "These," said Lenin, "are the lofty tasks that I dream of for our Workers' and Peasants' Inspection. This is why I am planning for it the amalgamation of the most authoritative Party body with an 'ordinary' People's Commissariat." These are the concluding words of the last article Lenin wrote.

Lenin, who always claimed to be an orthodox Marxist,

who no doubt did use the Marxist method in approaching social phenomena, and who saw the international question in class terms, approached the problems of government more like a chief executive of a strictly "elitist" turn of mind. He did not apply methods of social analysis to the government itself and was content to consider it purely in terms of organizational methods. This was simply the result of the situation of Soviet power at the beginning of 1923: political power, especially under the NEP, was practically the only instrument of action left to the Bolsheviks. This unexpected fact, which worried those who held this power, was the earliest manifestation of one of the most original characteristics of our time: the primacy of political factors, the control that governments possess over the economy and over society in general. Leninism was more apt than other schools of Marxism to grasp this truth because its voluntarism tended to emphasize political consciousness and the possibility of instilling it into the social forces from above.

Lenin's elitism, therefore, was merely an expression of his adaptation to a situation in which the driving force of the regime was an elite. His problem was how to use that elite in such a way that it would initiate the process of social transformation throughout the whole country. But in this sphere Lenin's thought contained certain weaknesses; he had failed to see the danger of the very tendencies that were soon to become so preponderant at the power summit.

It is true that in the circumstances prevailing at the end of 1921 it was quite understandable that Lenin's main concern should be the preservation of the power that had been acquired at the price of such sacrifice, rather than the organization of safeguards against the abuse of that power and against the hypertrophy of the dictatorship. The question should have occurred to him in 1922, but it escaped his attention, as did the national question, "almost completely," as he was later to admit. Lenin, who had become the prisoner of his illness, but also of his own government machine, turned at last to the difficult and perhaps in the short run insoluble problem of how to guarantee the political and moral health of the dictatorship. The social forces that should be participating effectively in its functioning could not be depended on because, first of all, they had to be educated. The workers, in particular, "would like to build a better apparatus for us, but they do not know how. . . . They have not yet developed the culture required for this."[4] As for the peasants, they must themselves be watched. This was why Lenin was strongly opposed to anything that savored, however remotely, of bourgeois democracy. He might have benefitted from further thought on this matter, but in the immediate situation, any recourse to democratic practice would have soon led to the eviction of the Bolsheviks from power. So he returned to his idea of an elite, to the quality of his men, until such time as the country had acquired an adequate level of culture.

If the whole structure thus rested on an "idealist" basis, on the quality of the senior cadres, and not on the power and consciousness of the working class, this attitude, however precarious and however unexpected in a Marxist, corresponded perfectly to the situation that Lenin had to face. Later other countries were confronted with similar structural problems and attempted the same solution. In this respect, Lenin's "Testament," by proposing a policy of governmental cadres, is still of interest today. But a more extensive and

---

[4] *Soch.*, Vol. XLV, pp. 390–91. The first version of the writings on the RKI says that the workers represent the basic strength of the new Central Committee and Central Control Commission. The article published in *Pravda* already says less about this. In "Better Fewer, But Better," the idea that workers should form a majority in the new institutions is completely abandoned.

deeper analysis must be made of the other aspect of the reality of power, the bureaucracy, which is a major problem for all developing countries that have chosen highly centralized and state-dominated systems.

Lenin was an ardent opponent of bureaucratism, but he did not analyze it sufficiently in depth. He admitted that as yet he did not fully understand the phenomenon: it is "a question that we have not yet been able to study."[5] As a rule, Lenin tended to see it as an inheritance from the old regime. This explanation, while true in part, is inadequate. Moreover, the bureaucracy was to become so inextricably a part of Soviet society and so deeply entrenched in the Soviet system, because of its composition and its methods, that the elements from the past were soon to lose all importance. The explanation must be sought elsewhere.

The continual increase in the number of civil servants and in their hold on the life of the country was facilitated by a conjunction of factors inherent in a backward country that had a real need for new administrative bodies and additional administrators, if it was to develop the economy along planned, centralist lines. But this meant—and Lenin did not realize it—that the bureaucracy would become the true social basis of power. There is no such thing as "pure" political power, devoid of any social foundation. A regime must find some other social basis than the apparatus of repression itself. The "void" in which the Soviet regime had seemed to be suspended had soon been filled, even if the Bolsheviks had not seen it, or did not wish to see it. The Stalinist period might be defined, therefore, as the substitution of the bureaucracy for the original social basis of the regime, namely,

[5] *Ibid.*, p. 251.

the working class, a section of the poorest peasants and certain strata of the intelligentsia.

Stalin, like Lenin, was a technician of power, but lacking Lenin's intellectual and moral stature and the scruples of "the Party's European cadres," he was quite willing to incorporate into his own plans all Lenin's amendments of an idealistic, internationalist, or socialist kind, knowing that a great many things would remain on paper and that reality, as he conceived it, would gain the upper hand. Thus all the projects to which Lenin attached so much importance—the enlargement of the Central Committee, the creation of a new Central Control Commission and its fusion with the RKI—would be accepted and put into practice; but since they would not be animated by the spirit in which they had been conceived, they would merely contribute to the triumph of the very tendencies Lenin wanted to combat.

If in the end Lenin's regime came to be based on a force, the bureaucracy, which he abhorred, it was only the result of a situation in which a program of development is imposed by a new regime on a backward country whose vital social forces are either weak, indifferent, or hostile. Lenin did not foresee this phenomenon because his social analysis was based on only three social classes—the workers, the peasants and the bourgeoisie—without taking any account of the state apparatus as a distinct social element in a country that had nationalized the main sectors of the economy. A great historian reproaches Lenin for not understanding the role of the administrative machine in a modern society, or rather, in a society in the process of becoming modernized.[6] This reproach is justified to the extent that Lenin confused the bureaucratic machine with the rule of the Tsarist-type

[6] Carr, *Socialism in One Country,* Vol. II, p. 200.

chinovnichestvo. But he had already dealt with the question in 1918, when he came out in favor of the administration against the anarchosyndicalist tendencies of the workers; in 1923, his plans for reorganization show that he was increasingly aware of the problem.

This time he approached it from another angle. Lenin continued to analyze the Party as the "vanguard of the proletariat." But it was composed of a minority of workers, a minority moreover that did not even play the leading role, and this worried Lenin considerably. The composition of the Party reflected more or less the state of the country's social forces. At its center, as in the regime as a whole, the general tendency was to bureaucratization—which would later increase its "monolithic" character. This was particularly apparent in the preponderance of executive functions and in the pyramidal structure of the apparatus. The process was that of the transformation of a political party into a state apparatus. Stalin seized on this tendency and, instead of controlling it as Lenin wished, accepted it, based his own power upon it and developed it.

At the end of his life, Lenin saw all these problems more and more clearly, for the intention, either implicit or explicit, of all his projects was to counteract the tendencies that were appearing in the regime and would triumph after his death. He would have had to live on to prove that he could have changed anything very substantially, but in that event he would also have had to overcome certain weaknesses in his analysis and reasoning; the phenomena he speaks of in his "Testament" were not yet very clear to him.

We see for example that the CCC-RKI that he proposed would have to be independent of the other organs at the summit of the governmental structure. In theory, this was guaranteed by its direct link with the Party Congress and by the fact that it was responsible exclusively to that assembly. But Lenin does not devote a single word to the Congress and its role. This is an important gap. This may be because, until then, the Congress had always enjoyed a position of sufficient importance and prestige. But without Lenin wishing it, the authority of the Congress had become considerably reduced by his promulgations of March 1921 on the prohibition of factions. This turned out to be a considerable weapon in the hands of the Secretariat, which by branding all disagreement as factional successfully stifled all real discussion and criticism. Moreover, the Congress was incapacitated by the Secretariat's power to appoint practically all the holders of responsible posts in the Party. Soon even the composition of the Congress itself would be freely manipulated by the Secretariat.

In these conditions, the freedom necessary for the true formulation of policy had disappeared. The mechanism that made it possible to change a line of policy, or an officeholder, had broken down; Lenin says nothing about it. Another serious gap was that the members of the future CCC-RKI were not to be elected, but appointed by the Orgburo. The whole fate of the reform depended therefore on the criteria and spirit of this selection. Unconsciously, Lenin continued to reason as if he would still be there. He realized that one member of the Politburo, the Gensek, possessed a power that the others did not have and he wanted the controllers to be able to supervise the activities of both the Gensek and the bureau. But if the Gensek retained his prerogatives—and Lenin proposes nothing explicitly to alter this situation, except to change the holder of the post—it would be he, in practice, who chose his own controllers. And that is exactly what happened.

Another very different gap, but a highly significant one,

was that the whole of Lenin's program was aimed at maintaining the unity of the Party and avoiding a split. But he says nothing of the phenomenon—factionism—that was to serve as a perpetual pretext for every attempt to stifle criticism. Under Stalin, the Central Control Commission, while apparently constituted according to Lenin's wishes, was to make this its almost sole preoccupation. It is quite possible that Lenin no longer thought factionism as dangerous as at the time of the Kronstadt uprising and was willing to abandon the secret clauses decided on at the Tenth Congress. This supposition certainly accords with the general tenor of the "Testament," as I shall try to show in the concluding chapter of this book.

10

IF
LENIN
HAD
LIVED...

In view of the almost negligible influence that Lenin's suggestions have actually had on events in the USSR, it might be tempting to conclude that they were merely utopian, detached from reality, or ineffective. In my opinion, they deserve more attention and a more positive appreciation. Although Lenin turned an objective eye on the problems of his regime, it is true that certain tendencies became apparent to him only at the very end of his life and others were imperfectly understood. Nevertheless, his proposals for reform represent, both in their explicit content and in their implicit

consequences, a total response to the political realities of
the country.

A brief review of these points would perhaps be useful at
this stage.

Lenin did not realize the full extent of the danger of a possible abuse of power at the summit of the hierarchy and of its
degeneration into an irresponsible personal dictatorship. But
he did perceive the problem in relation to a particular aspect
of the political life of the country, the question of nationalities. Indeed, he was so alarmed by what he saw that he was
prepared to have the structure of the Union, which had just
been adopted by the Congress of the Soviets, annulled and to
demand the political liquidation of the *dzerzhimordy*. When
one thinks of the positions adopted, two years after Lenin's
death, by the three leading *dzerzhimordy,* one is struck by
the enormous gulf between the subsequent course of events
and the direction Lenin wished them to take. Instead of
being expelled from the Party, Ordzhonikidze was in charge
of the control apparatus of the Party and the state, Dzerzhinsky was chairman of the National Economic Council, and
Stalin still held the key post in the Party.

The idea of the Central Control Commission was not
merely a means of improving the work of the state apparatus.
Its formation would involve important changes in the very
character of the leadership and of the ruling elite within the
Party. If the enlargement of the Central Committee had been
carried out, it would have meant that the Secretariat and the
entire Party executive would have been subject to the control
of a wider, more representative body. With their entry into
the highest organs of Party government, a new role would
have been given to the specialists and scientists—and Lenin
wanted it to be a dominant one. From the initial idea of giving greater authority to the decisions of the Gosplan, Lenin

had developed a CCC-RKI that would educate the *tsekisty* and assist them in the task of reforming the apparatus. If this spectacular effort to gather around the Central Committee "all that is best in the dictatorship" had really been undertaken, the quality of the personnel at the summit of power, its methods of work and its internal relations would have been transformed. Even if it had not succeeded, at least a serious attempt would have been made to counteract the tendencies within the apparatus. Moreover, these changes seemed especially suited to the character of the new period that was then beginning—a period, according to Lenin, of respite. The specter of famine, which had been particularly terrifying in the years 1920 and 1921, receded with the first good harvest, that of 1922, produced under the NEP. The country could now pass on to those tasks of construction and culture (in the dynamic sense of *kulturnichestvo*) that could not be completed within a specific time limit. This work in depth would obviously necessitate (though this was not stated explicitly) not only an evolution in the methods and style of the government, but also the replacement at the summit of the somewhat crude and uneducated *apparatchiki* by cultured and specialized administrators and politicians. It would also mean a shift of the center of gravity away from the Secretariat towards the Central Committee. Lenin's project was virtually a *coup d'état,* since it involved the removal of certain leaders and the introduction of a new orientation in the whole functioning of the dictatorship—in methods of recruitment and work and in new criteria for the choice of objectives. It would be tempting to use a now fashionable term and speak of a "technocratic revolution" against a bureaucracy that he regarded as too primitive.

On the other hand, Lenin was trying to establish at the summit of the dictatorship a balance between different elements, a system of reciprocal control that could serve the same function—the comparison is no more than approximate—as the separation of powers in a democratic regime. An important Central Committee, raised to the rank of Party Conference, would lay down the broad lines of policy and supervise the whole Party apparatus, while itself participating in the execution of the more important tasks, both as a body and through the activities of its individual members. Part of this Central Committee, the Central Control Commission, would, in addition to its work within the Central Committee, act as a control of the Central Committee and of its various offshoots—the Political Bureau, the Secretariat, the Orgburo. The Central Control Commission, with its specialists from the RKI or the CCC-RKI, would occupy a special position with relation to the other institutions; its independence would be assured by its direct link to the Party Congress, without the mediation of the Politburo and its administrative organs or of the Central Committee. Seen in this way, these projects seem complex but not very highly developed. But even if they were merely embryonic, they do acknowledge the problem of principle: how to assure the survival of a revolutionary dictatorship established in "premature" conditions and at the same time safeguard its original purity and devotion to principle. Lenin tried to rationalize the dictatorship in such a way that it could protect itself both from external enemies and from the dangers inherent in dictatorial power.

The most explicit part of Lenin's "Testament" might be summed up in these three commandments:

1. Combat nationalism, especially Russian nationalism—that Great Power chauvinism that the whole government machine tends to serve; strive to inculcate an internationalist spirit into the peoples of the Union.

2. Combat an ignorant, wasteful and potentially oppressive bureaucracy at every level, including the Party leadership; strive to create an efficient state administration.

3. Remove Stalin.

The absence, in the "Testament," of any mention of the prohibition of factions is made all the more significant by the fact that there is also no mention of terror as a means of promoting the execution of the government's plans. Terror had occupied a fairly considerable place in Lenin's earlier writings, and he had always defended it as an ultimate weapon. The new Volume XLV of the *Works* includes a number of writings that had previously been either unknown or little known in which Lenin analyzes terror as a method. It was a weapon that must always be held in reserve, Lenin reminds his readers, especially as the liberalization brought about by the NEP would tend to weaken the security of the state. In a letter to Kamenev that appeared for the first time in 1959, he declares: "It is a great mistake to think that the NEP put an end to terror; we shall again have recourse to terror and to economic terror."[1] He explains to Kamenev that a means must be found whereby all those who would now like to go beyond the limits assigned to businessmen by the state could be reminded "tactfully and politely" of the existence of this ultimate weapon.

But in other writings, which are more disturbing in view of the use to which they were later put, Lenin went further. In his amendments to the project for the penal code, he insisted that the notion of "counterrevolutionary activity" should be given the widest possible interpretation. This definition was to be linked with the "international bourgeoisie" in such a

[1] Letter to Kamenev, March 3, 1922 (*Soch.,* Vol. XLIV, p. 428).

way that this kind of crime became quite imprecise from a juridical point of view and thus left the way wide open for every kind of arbitrary action. Among other things, the crime would cover "propaganda and agitation" and "participation in or aid to an organization" which might benefit that part of the international bourgeoisie that does not recognize the Soviet regime's equal rights with capitalist states and seeks to overthrow it by force. This definition was already broad enough, but what was worse, in view of the fact that the crime could carry capital punishment, was that it could be extended by analogy. Whoever "gave help objectively to that part of the international bourgeoisie" (which actively opposed the regime), and similarly whoever belonged to an organization within the country whose activities "might assist or be capable of assisting" this bourgeoisie, would also be guilty![2] This case shows that at this time Lenin was anxious to leave room for the use of terror or the threat of its use (not through the Cheka alone but through tribunals and a regular procedure) as long as the big capitalist countries continued to threaten the USSR.

Lenin, then, was very far from being a weak liberal, incapable of taking resolute action when necessary. But unlike some of his successors, he hated repression; for him, it should be used only in the defense of the regime against serious threat and as a punishment for those who contravened legality.

But to return to Lenin's last program, the use of constraint —let alone terror—is ostensibly excluded in establishing the foundations of a new society. Lenin's second *What Is To Be Done?* pleads for caution, restraint, moderation and patience.

---

[2] Letter to Kursky, Commissar of Justice, May 15, 1922 (*Soch.*, Vol. XLV, pp. 189–90).

Lenin has not abandoned the use of constraint in the defense
of the regime, but for purposes of construction all undue
haste is forbidden: "We must show sound skepticism for too
rapid progress, for boastfulness, etc."—these words are taken
from "Better Fewer, But Better." "Better get good human
material in two or even three years than work in haste without
hope of getting any at all." "No second revolution!"—this was
to be the interpretation of the "Testament" that Bukharin,
five years later, was to throw back at Stalin, and he was right.
Lenin no longer described force as the "midwife of a new
society" after the seizure of power and the return of peace;
the new rule in this new situation was clearly that of gradual
evolution. And this rule was formulated against the whole
pressure of Russian realities, which—as Lenin was very well
aware—tended in the opposite direction.

The rule "Better fewer, but better" would be difficult to
observe, but Lenin refuses, in advance, the argument of
spontaneous tendencies: "I know that the opposite rule will
force its way through a thousand loopholes. I know that
enormous resistance will have to be put up, that devilish
persistence will be required, that in the first few years at least
work in this field will be hellishly hard. Nevertheless, I am
convinced that only by achieving this aim shall we create a
republic that is really worthy of the name of Soviet, socialist,
and so on, and so forth."[3]

In my opinion, one can hardly describe Lenin's great
objectives as utopian. Many of the objectives assigned to the
regime in the fields of economic and cultural development
have been attained. The other grand design, that of creating
a dictatorial machine capable of controlling itself to a large
degree, seems closer today, but only after an initial cata-

[3] *Ibid.,* p. 392. See Appendix IX.

strophic failure: the Soviet regime underwent a long period of "Stalinism," which in its basic features was diametrically opposed to the recommendations of the "Testament." This fact requires some elucidation. Left-wing dictatorship is one of the most significant political phenomena of our time. Its role is an important one and its prospects of development are far from exhausted. But there is no evidence that this type of dictatorship, at a certain stage in its development, must of necessity and in every case degenerate into a personal, despotic and irrational dictatorship. From a historical point of view, there was nothing essentially utopian about Lenin's aim of achieving a rational dictatorial regime, with men of integrity at its head and efficient institutions working consciously to go beyond both underdevelopment and dictatorship. Moreover, in Lenin's own time, and in extremely difficult conditions, the Soviet dictatorial machine still functioned in a very different way from the one it was later to adopt. Lenin's plans were not put into practice because the tendencies that had emerged from the civil war could only be counteracted by daring reforms, and in the absence of a capable and undisputed leader the plans in question remained no more than mere "wishes." The machine that had been set up under Lenin found no difficulty in bypassing the dead leader's most earnest wishes; the embalming of his corpse and the posthumous cult of his person helped to dissimulate a type of dictatorship utterly foreign to his plans.

The greatest discrepancy between Lenin's intentions and actual history is to be found in the field of methods. It would appear today that the USSR has entered a period of internal development in which economic and educative methods are being gradually substituted for administrative constraint, as Lenin wished. But for a long time terror was the main instrument in the establishment of the new structures.

In our time a good deal of discussion is taking place as to whether Stalin's methods, which have proved so prejudicial to the general idea of socialism and to the development of the socialist movement in the world, were the brutal but correct choice of the only possible way, or whether there existed another formula that Stalin was personally incapable of conceiving.

No one doubts that there were powerful forces inherent in Russia's internal situation and international position that encouraged recourse to strong-arm methods in overcoming the obstacles to development, which were extremely persistent in this backward, agrarian and isolated country. No one doubts either that, whatever the ability of her leaders and elites may have been, Soviet Russia was bound to undergo crises and upheavals. A curve of development rising gently and gradually, without sudden dips, was difficult to imagine. Lenin was under no illusions on that score and did nothing to foster them. What he did want, however, in all circumstances, was a considered policy; he wanted the country to keep its head whatever conflict or dilemma it might find itself in. If he had lived, he would inevitably have had to solve the problem of "primitive accumulation" (the creation of the initial capital for the launching of the industrial economy), whatever his aversion to such a concept. He would have had to act when the peasantry, even without any consciously hostile political motives, refused to sell its grain and practically threatened to starve the country, because of the feeble supply of industrial products. He would have been constantly confronted by the paradox of a single party in a socially diversified country. He would have had to preserve the unity of the Party and the requirements of discipline and efficiency, which were so often in contradiction with the freedom of criticism necessary if the Party was not to fall into bureaucratic degeneration.

Would Lenin in fact have succeeded in solving all these questions correctly, and how would he have gone about doing so? (The question might arise whether a historian may legitimately concern himself with such hypotheses. I believe that he may, on condition that he does not exceed certain limits. If he does exceed these limits, then of course his work becomes gratuitous speculation.)

In answering this question, we must proceed to an extrapolation whose point of departure is to be found in our knowledge of Lenin's character and of his last program. There can be little doubt that Lenin would have set about the realization of his reforms; as he did so, some of them would have proved unrealistic or impracticable and would have been replaced. Others, and even perhaps his entire policy, would have met with opposition from within the Party and with practical difficulties in the country at large. The internal opposition would have come from the bureaucracy, the *apparatchiki* appointed by the Orgburo. But this opposition would have been weakened, at least temporarily, by the removal of the Stalin group, as Lenin had intended. Under Lenin, there would have been no letup in the struggle against "administrative methods" and the inefficiency of the bureaucracy and against Russian nationalism (and the local nationalisms that it helped to keep alive). He would have been constantly obliged to organize support both within and outside the Party. He would have had to appeal to the active and morally sensitive elements in the country: young workers and students; intellectuals; the best elements in the peasantry; certain elements of the Revolutionary Old Guard, of other socialist parties and of other groups, according to the circumstances; the Bolshevik Old Guard, composed of men who were then still young; the more enlightened administrative elements would also have provided support. The *apparatchiki,* the police, the *dzerzhimordy* and the *chinovniki* could never, of course, have disappeared completely, but they would have been constantly attacked, demoralized and repressed. The front of the stage would have been occupied by the many militants that Stalin was to eliminate, and also by the more narrow-minded but often honest militants who were to be used by the Stalinist system, and by all kinds of valuable nonmembers who were to perish in the purges. It is easier to imagine Lenin himself perishing in prison than inflicting such an insane hemorrhage on his country. A coalition of Lenin with Trotsky and others would have enabled a rational use of the best cadres, instead of their elimination. Of course, this mass of individuals would not only have helped to carry out Lenin's program; they would also have been a seedbed of opposition that tried to outflank him sometimes from the left and sometimes from the right. But Lenin would certainly not have used Stalinist methods against them. On the other hand, it would be nothing more than speculation to affirm that Lenin would have succeeded without any doubt. He too might have succumbed and ended, like so many others, as a "deviationist." But what may be said with certainty is that he would have done his utmost to combat the processes that were to make the Stalinist period what it was.

In order not to be beaten, Lenin would have had to show quite extraordinary skill and daring as a political manipulator and innovator; he is known to have possessed these qualities in ample measure. He would have had, in his own words, to act with "devilish persistence." He was probably quite capable of it. It is legitimate to believe that Lenin, acting in concert with Trotsky and others, would have been able to bring Soviet Russia through a less tragic, more rational and, for the cause of socialism, less compromising path. In fact, Lenin needed Trotsky to realize his idea. It was not merely because of his illness that he called in Trotsky's assistance. The two men complemented each other very well, even if they would not have produced the symbiosis that Lenin had wanted between Krzhizhanovsky and Pyatakov at the Gosplan. Between them, they symbolized the motive force of the October Revolution.

Trotsky alone would not have been capable of carrying out the reorganization and consolidation and the preservation of those later to be purged. Deutscher explains very well why he could not be Lenin's "heir": when Lenin finally succumbed to paralysis, for example, he concluded the very kind of "rotten compromise" that Lenin had warned him against. He calmed Kamenev's fears by telling him that although he was in agreement with Lenin on fundamentals, he did not agree to "finishing with Stalin, or to expelling Ordzhonikidze, or to removing Dzerzhinsky from the Commissariat of Communications." He merely scolded Stalin, saying, "There should be no more intrigues, but honest cooperation."[4] He wanted to show magnanimity, believing that, with Lenin's support enshrined in the "Testament," he could afford to do so. This merely showed that he had not understood Lenin's essential recommendations.

He also had the weakness of a man who was too haughty and, in a sense, too idealistic to indulge in the political machinations inside the small group of leaders. His position as an outsider, on account of his past and his style, prevented him from acting when the moment came—for him, it only came once—with the necessary determination. He succumbed to a fetishization of the Party, to a certain legalism

---

[4] Trotsky, *My Life,* p. 486.

and to scruples that paralyzed him and prevented him from reacting unhesitantly, as Lenin would have done, to what his enemies were doing against him. As the founder, Lenin was not afraid of unmaking and remaking what he had made with his own hands. He was not afraid of organizing the people around him, of plotting, of fighting for the victory of his line and of keeping the situation under control.

Trotsky was not such a man. Lenin disappeared and Stalin was assured of victory.

APPENDIXES

I

STALIN'S "AUTONOMIZATION" PLAN

1. Consider the usefulness of an agreement between the Soviet Republics of the Ukraine, Byelorussia, Azerbaijan, Georgia and Armenia and the RSFSR concerning the formal adhesion of these Republics to the RSFSR, leaving aside the question of Bukhara, Khorezm and the Far Eastern Republic, and confining the agreement to the conclusion of protocols on customs duties, foreign trade, foreign affairs, military questions, etc.

Addenda: Make the necessary changes in the constitutions of the Republics listed in paragraph 1 and to that of the RSFSR after examination of the question by the Soviet organs.

2. As a result, the resolutions of the VTSIK[1] will be regarded as executory concerning the central institutions of the Republics listed in paragraph 1, and those of the SNKs[2] and of the STO[3] of the RSFSR for the unified commissariats of these Republics.

---

[1] All-Russian Central Executive Committee.
[2] Sovnarkom, the Council of People's Commissars.
[3] Council of Labor and Defense.

Addenda: The representatives of these Republics will sit in the presidium of the VTSIK and of the RSFSR.

3. The services of foreign affairs, foreign trade, defense, communications and posts and telegraphs of the Republics listed in paragraph 1 will be merged with the corresponding institutions of the RSFSR, and the corresponding commissariats of the RSFSR will send delegations of representatives into these Republics, accompanied by a small number of civil servants.

These representatives will be appointed by the commissariats of the RSFSR with the agreement of the TSIKs of the Republics.

The participation of the representatives of the Republics concerned in the commissariats of Foreign Affairs and Foreign Trade must be regarded as useful.

4. The commissariats of Finance, Food, Labor and Economics of the Republics will be strictly subject to the directives of the corresponding commissariats of the RSFSR.

5. The other commissariats of the Republics listed in paragraph 1, that is the commissariats of Justice, Education, the Interior, Agriculture, Workers' and Peasants' Control, Health and Social Insurance will be regarded as independent.

Addenda 1: The organizations of the Republics listed above concerned with the Counter-Revolutionary struggle will be subject to the directives of the GPU of the RSFSR.

Addenda 2: The TSIKs of the Republics will enjoy the right of amnesty only in civil affairs.

6. If this decision is confirmed by the Central Committee of the RCP, it will not be made public, but communicated to the Central Committees of the Republics for circulation among the Soviet organs, the Central Executive Committees

or the Congresses of the Soviets of the said Republics before the convocation of the All-Russian Congress of the Soviets, where it will be declared to be the wish of these Republics.

[Central Archives of the Party at the Institute of Marxism-Leninism of the CC-CPSU. Source: *Soch.,* Vol. XLV, pp. 557–58.]

II

LENIN'S COMMENTS AND HIS PROJECT FOR THE FORMATION OF THE USSR

Letter to L. B. Kamenev, for the members of the Political Bureau of the CC-RCP (b)
26/IX

Comrade Kamenev! You will no doubt have received from Stalin the resolution of his commission concerning the incorporation of the independent Republics in the RSFSR.

If you have not yet received it, please collect it from the secretary and read it immediately. I have already discussed it with Sokolnikov, spoken about it today with Stalin and will be seeing Mdivani (a Georgian Communist suspected of *nezavisimstvo*) tomorrow.

In my opinion, the question is of enormous importance. Stalin is in rather too much of a hurry. You must—since you did at one time intend to take up the question and have even studied it to some extent—think about it seriously and Zinoviev likewise.

Stalin has already agreed to make a concession, that of replacing the term "adhesion" to the RSFSR in paragraph 1 by "formal union with the RSFSR within the framework of a Union of the Soviet Republics of Europe and Asia."

I hope the significance of this concession is clear: we recognize that we are equals in law with the SSR of the Ukraine, etc. and join it on an equal footing in a new Union, a new Federation, the "Union of the Soviet Republics of Europe and Asia."

In this case, paragraph 2 must also be altered to create, parallel with the sessions of the VTSIK of the RSFSR, something in the nature of a "federal VTSIK of the Union of Soviet Republics of Europe and Asia."

If the first organization is to meet once a week and the second similarly (or even if they meet every two weeks), it will not be very difficult to combine their activities.

It is important not to give grist to the mill of the *nezavisimtsy*, not to destroy their *independence*, but to establish a *new echelon*, a Federation of Republics *with equal rights*.

The second part of paragraph 2 could remain unchanged: complaints (against the decisions of the STO and the SNK) will be examined by the federal VTSIK, *without delaying execution however* (as for the RSFSR).

Paragraph 3 could stand with this alteration: "will be merged into federal commissariats situated in Moscow, the corresponding commissariats of the RSFSR having accredited representatives and a small number of civil servants in the *member Republics of the Union of the Republics of Europe and Asia.*"

The second part of paragraph 3 remains unchanged; it might be better, in order to be more equitable, to say "after agreement with the VTSIK of the member republics of the Union of Soviet Republics of Europe and Asia."

We should also give more thought to the third part: should not "useful" be replaced by "*obligatory*"? Should we not stipulate a *conditional* obligation, if only in the form of an *interpellation* and to accept decisions not subject to interpellation only in "exceptional" cases?

Paragraph 4 should perhaps stipulate "merged after agreement with the VTSIKs."

In paragraph 5 we might add "with the creation of common (or general) conferences and congresses of a *purely consultative* (or *no more than consultative*) character."

This would involve corresponding changes in the first and second addenda.

Stalin has agreed to delay presenting the resolution to the Political Bureau of the Central Committee until my arrival. I shall arrive on Monday, October 2. I should like to see you with Rykov for a couple of hours in the morning, between noon and two o'clock, say, or, if necessary, in the evening, say from 5 to 7 or from 6 to 8.

This, then, is my initial project. I shall make any further additions or alterations after my discussions with Mdivani and the other comrades. I would urge you to do likewise and send me your reply.

Yours,
LENIN

P.S. Send copies to all the members of the Political Bureau.

[Written September 26, 1922, and published from the manuscript. First published in 1959 in the *Leninskii Sbornik* (Moscow, Institute of Marxism-Leninism, 1924–1959), Vol. XXXVI. Source: *Soch.*, Vol. XLV, pp. 211–13.]

III

THE PROJECT SUBMITTED TO THE CENTRAL COMMITTEE ON OCTOBER 6, 1922, DRAWN UP BY STALIN AND INCORPORATING LENIN'S AMENDMENTS

1. Consider as indispensable the conclusion of an agreement between the Ukraine, Byelorussia, the Federation of Transcaucasian Republics and the RSFSR concerning union within the framework of a "Union of Soviet Socialist Republics," each of them possessing the right to leave the "Union" of its own accord.

2. The supreme body of the "Union" will be the "Federal TSIK," formed by the representatives of the TSIKs of the RSFSR, the Transcaucasian Federation, the Ukraine and Byelorussia, represented proportionally to their population.

3. The executive organ of the "Federal TSIK," will be the "Federal Sovnarkom," to be appointed by the "Federal TSIK."

4. The commissariats of Foreign Affairs, Foreign Trade, Defense, Communications and Posts and Telegraphs of the Republics and of the Federation forming the "Union" will be merged with the corresponding organs of the USSR, the corresponding commissariats of the "Union of Republics" having in all the Republics and Federations their accredited representatives and a small number of civil servants, ap-

pointed by the commissariats of the "Union" with the agreement of the TSIKs of the Federations and Republics.

Addenda: Consider as indispensable the adjunction of representatives of the Republics concerned to the representations abroad of the commissariats of Foreign Affairs and Foreign Trade.

5. The commissariats of Finance, Food, Economics, Labor and Control of the member Republics and Federations of the "Union of Republics," as well as their central organs concerned with the counterrevolutionary struggle, will be subject to the directives of the corresponding commissariats and to the decisions of the Sovnarkom and STO of the "Union of Republics."

6. The other commissariats of the member Republics of the Union, that is the commissariats of Justice, Education, the Interior, Agriculture, Health and Social Insurance, will be regarded as independent.

[Central Archives of the Party at the Institute of Marxism-Leninism of the CC-CPSU. Source: *Soch.,* Vol. XLV, p. 559.]

IV

STALIN'S OPINION OF LENINS' LETTER OF OCTOBER 13 CONCERNING THE MONOPOLY OF FOREIGN TRADE

Comrade Lenin's letter has not made me change my mind as to the correctness of the decision of the plenum of the

Central Committee of October 6 concerning foreign trade. The "millions" of the Commissariat of Foreign Trade (the figures, incidentally, must first be established and calculations made) lose all value if one takes into account the fact that they are compensated for several times over by the tens of thousands in gold that this commissariat takes out of Russia. Nevertheless, in view of the insistent character of Comrade Lenin's proposal to adjourn the execution of the decision of the plenum of the Central Committee, I vote for, in order that this question may be discussed by the next plenum, with Lenin's participation.

[Central Archives of the Party at the Institute of Marxism-Leninism of the CC-CPSU. Source: Fotieva, *Iz Vospominaniy*, pp. 28–29.]

V

KRUPSKAYA'S LETTER TO KAMENEV OF DECEMBER 23, 1922, CONCERNING STALIN'S BEHAVIOR TOWARDS HER

Lev Borisovich! Stalin subjected me to a storm of the coarsest abuse yesterday about a brief note that Lenin dictated to me, with the permission of the doctors. I didn't join the Party yesterday. In the whole of these last thirty years I have never heard a single coarse word from a comrade. The interests of the Party and of Ilich are no less dear to me than to Stalin. At the moment I need all the self-control I can muster. I know better than all the doctors what can and what cannot be said to Ilich, for I know what disturbs him and what doesn't, and in any case I know this better than Stalin.

[Krupskaya asks (it is the editors who summarize without quoting) to be protected "from gross interference in her private life, unworthy abuse and threats." She continues:]

I have no doubt as to the unanimous decision of the Control Commission with which Stalin takes it upon himself to threaten me, but I have neither the time nor the energy to lose in such a stupid farce. I too am human and my nerves are at breaking-point. N. Krupskaya.

[Same archives. Source: *Soch.,* Vol. LIV, pp. 674–75.]

VI

ON DECEMBER 24 THE POLITICAL BUREAU GIVES LENIN PERMISSION TO DICTATE HIS NOTES

1. Vladimir Ilich is granted permission to dictate for five to ten minutes a day, but it ought not to have the character of a correspondence and Ilich must not expect replies to these notes. Visits are forbidden.

2. Friends and servants are forbidden to communicate anything to Lenin concerning political life, in order not to give him cause for reflection and anxiety.

[Same archives. Source: *Soch.,* Vol. XLV, p. 710.]

VII

WORK SCHEDULE DICTATED BY LENIN ON DECEMBER 27 (OR 28), 1922

Memorandum:

In the letter on the increase in the number of members of the Central Committee a paragraph has been omitted on the relations between the enlarged Central Committee and the Workers' and Peasants' Inspection.

Subjects to consider:

1. The Tsentrosoyuz[1] and its importance from the point of view of the NEP.

2. The relation between the Glavprofobr[2] and the work of people's education in general.

3. The national question and internationalism (in relation to the recent conflict in the Georgian Party).

4. The new book of statistics on national education published in 1922.

[Source: *Soch.*, Vol. XLV, p. 592.]

[1] Cooperative Consumer Union.
[2] Committee of Vocational Education.

VIII

TROTSKY'S REPLY TO LENIN CONCERNING THE DEFENSE OF THE GEORGIANS

The Institute of Marxism-Leninism at Moscow says that Trotsky refused to take on the defense of the Georgians before the Central Committee and the Congress under the pretext that he was ill. No proof is provided to support this allegation, which is repeated by Louis Fischer in his biography of Lenin. But Deutscher says the opposite[1] and the "Journal" mentions, on March 6, 1923, that "the reply [Trotsky's] was received by telephone and taken down in shorthand." If this reply had been negative, Lenin would not have sent Trotsky the text of his memorandum and the copy of the letter to the Georgians that was written after receiving Trotsky's reply.

We also possess a letter from Fotieva to Kamenev, dated April 16, 1923, which confirms Trotsky's acceptance. Here is the letter:[2]

"To Comrade Kamenev (copy to Comrade Trotsky):

Leon Borisovich:

Supplementing our telephone conversation, I communi-

---

[1] Cf. *Soch.*, Vol. XLV, p. 607; Fischer, *The Life of Lenin* (New York, Harper & Row, Publishers, 1964), p. 671; Deutscher, *The Prophet Unarmed.*

[2] Letter quoted by Trotsky, *Stalin School of Falsification*, p. 73. My italics.

cated to you as acting chairman of the Political Bureau the following:

As I already told you, December 31, 1922, Vladimir Ilich dictated an article on the national question.

This question has worried him extremely and he was preparing to speak on it at the party congress. Not long before his last illness he told me that he would publish this article, but later. After that he took sick without giving final directions.

Vladimir Ilich considered this article to be a guiding one and extremely important. At his direction it was communicated to *comrade Trotsky whom Vladimir Ilich authorized to defend his point of view upon the given question. . . .*"

The Institute of Marxism-Leninism does not quote this letter, but confirms its existence and states that Fotieva sent it to the Political Bureau on April 16, 1923.

IX

"BETTER FEWER, BUT BETTER"
(*Pravda,* March 4, 1923)

In the matter of improving our state apparatus, the Workers' and Peasants' Inspection should not, in my opinion, either strive after quantity or hurry. We have so far been able to devote so little thought and attention to the efficiency of our state apparatus that it would now be quite legitimate if we took special care to secure its thorough organization, and concentrated in the Workers' and Peasants' Inspection a staff of workers really abreast of the times, i.e., not inferior to the best West European standards. For a socialist republic this condition is, of course, too modest. But our experience of the first five years has fairly crammed our heads with mistrust and skepticism. These qualities assert themselves involuntarily when, for example, we hear people dilating at too great length and too flippantly on "proletarian" culture. For a start, we should be satisfied with real bourgeois culture; for a start, we should be glad to dispense with the cruder types of pre-bourgeois culture, i.e., bureaucratic culture or serf culture, etc. In matters of culture, haste and sweeping measures are most harmful. Many of our young writers and Communists should get this well into their heads.

Thus, in the matter of our state apparatus we should now draw the conclusion from our past experience that it would be better to proceed more slowly.

Our state apparatus is so deplorable, not to say wretched, that we must first think very carefully how to combat its defects, bearing in mind that these defects are rooted in the past, which, although it has been overthrown, has not yet been overcome, has not yet reached the stage of a culture that has receded into the distant past. I say culture deliberately, because in these matters we can only regard as achieved what has become part and parcel of our culture, of our social life, our habits. We might say that the good in our social system has not been properly studied, understood, and taken to heart; it has been hastily grasped at; it has not been verified or tested, corroborated by experience, and not made durable, etc. Of course, it could not be otherwise in a revolutionary epoch, when development proceeded at such breakneck speed that in a matter of five years we passed from tsarism to the Soviet system.

It is time we did something about it. We must show sound skepticism for too rapid progress, for boastfulness, etc. We must give thought to testing the steps forward we proclaim every hour, take every minute and then prove every second that they are flimsy, superficial and misunderstood. The most harmful thing here would be haste. The most harmful thing would be to rely on the assumption that we know at least something, or that we have any considerable number of elements necessary for the building of a really new state apparatus, one really worthy to be called socialist, Soviet, etc.

No, we are ridiculously deficient of such an apparatus, and even of the elements of it, and we must remember that we should not stint time on building it, and that it will take many, many years.

What elements have we for building this apparatus? Only two. First, the workers who are absorbed in the struggle for socialism. These elements are not sufficiently educated. They would like to build a better apparatus for us, but they do not know how. They cannot build one. They have not yet developed the culture required for this; and it is culture that is required. Nothing will be achieved in this by doing things in a rush, by assault, by vim or vigor, or in general, by way of the best human qualities. Secondly, we have elements of knowledge, education and training, but they are ridiculously inadequate compared with all other countries.

Here we must not forget that we are too prone to compensate (or imagine that we can compensate) our lack of knowledge by zeal, haste, etc.

In order to renovate our state apparatus we must at all costs set out, first, to learn, secondly, to learn, and thirdly, to learn, and then see to it that learning shall not remain a dead letter, or a fashionable catchphrase (and we should admit in all frankness that this happens very often with us), that learning shall really become part of our very being, that it shall actually and fully become a constituent element of our social life. In short, we must not make the demands that are made by bourgeois Western Europe, but demands that are fit and proper for a country which has set out to develop into a socialist country.

The conclusions to be drawn from the above are the following: we must make the Workers' and Peasants' Inspection a really exemplary institution, an instrument to improve our state apparatus.

In order that it may attain the desired high level, we must follow the rule: "Measure your cloth seven times before you cut."

For this purpose, we must utilize the very best of what there is in our social system, and utilize it with the greatest caution, thoughtfulness and knowledge, to build up the new People's Commissariat.

For this purpose, the best elements that we have in our social system—such as, first, the advanced workers, and, second, the really enlightened elements for whom we can vouch that they will not take the word for the deed, and will not utter a single word that goes against their conscience—should not shrink from admitting any difficulty and should not shrink from any struggle in order to achieve the object they have seriously set themselves.

We have been bustling for five years trying to improve our state apparatus, but it has been mere bustle, which has proved useless in these five years, or even futile, or even harmful. This bustle created the impression that we were doing something, but in effect it was only clogging up our institutions and our brains.

It is high time things were changed.

We must follow the rule: Better fewer, but better. We must follow the rule: Better get good human material in

two or even three years than work in haste without hope of
getting any at all.

I know that it will be hard to keep to this rule and apply
it under our conditions. I know that the opposite rule will
force its way through a thousand loopholes. I know that
enormous resistance will have to be put up, that devilish persistence will be required, that in the first few years at least
work in this field will be hellishly hard. Nevertheless, I am
convinced that only by such effort shall we be able to achieve
our aim; and that only by achieving this aim shall we create
a republic that is really worthy of the name of Soviet, socialist, and so on, and so forth.

Many readers probably thought that the figures I quoted
by way of illustration in my first article were too small. I am
sure that many calculations may be made to prove that they
are. But I think that we must put one thing above all such and
other calculations, i.e., our desire to obtain really exemplary
quality.

I think that the time has at last come when we must work
in real earnest to improve our state apparatus, and in this
there can scarcely be anything more harmful than haste.
That is why I would sound a strong warning against inflating
the figures. In my opinion, we should, on the contrary, be
especially sparing with figures in this matter. Let us say
frankly that the People's Commissariat of the Workers' and
Peasants' Inspection does not at present enjoy the slightest
authority. Everybody knows that no other institutions are
worse organized than those of our Workers' and Peasants'
Inspection, and that under present conditions nothing can
be expected from this People's Commissariat. We must have
this firmly fixed in our minds if we really want to create
within a few years an institution that will, first, be an exemplary institution, secondly, win everybody's absolute con-

fidence, and, thirdly, prove to all and sundry that we have really justified the work of such a highly placed institution as the Central Control Commission. In my opinion, we must immediately and irrevocably reject all general figures for the size of office staffs. We must select employees for the Workers' and Peasants' Inspection with particular care and only on the basis of the strictest test. Indeed, what is the use of establishing a People's Commissariat which carries on anyhow, which does not enjoy the slightest confidence, and whose word carries scarcely any weight? I think that our main object in launching the work of reconstruction that we now have in mind is to avoid all this.

The workers whom we are enlisting as members of the Central Control Commission must be irreproachable Communists, and I think that a great deal has yet to be done to teach them the methods and objects of their work. Furthermore, there must be a definite number of secretaries to assist in this work, who must be put to a triple test before they are appointed to their posts. Lastly, the officials whom in exceptional cases we shall accept directly as employees of the Workers' and Peasants' Inspection must conform to the following requirements:

First, they must be recommended by several Communists.

Second, they must pass a test for knowledge of our state apparatus.

Third, they must pass a test in the fundamentals of the theory of our state apparatus, in the fundamentals of management, office routine, etc.

Fourth, they must work in such close harmony with the members of the Central Control Commission and with their own secretariat that we could vouch for the work of the whole apparatus.

I know that these requirements are extraordinarily strict,

and I am very much afraid that the majority of the "practical" workers in the Workers' and Peasants' Inspection will say that these requirements are impracticable, or will scoff at them. But I ask any of the present chiefs of the Workers' and Peasants' Inspection, or anyone associated with that body, whether they can honestly tell me the practical purpose of a People's Commissariat like the Workers' and Peasants' Inspection. I think this question will help them recover their sense of proportion. Either it is not worthwhile having another of the numerous reorganizations that we have had of this hopeless affair, the Workers' and Peasants' Inspection, or we must really set to work, by slow, difficult and unusual methods, and by testing these methods over and over again, to create something really exemplary, something that will win the respect of all and sundry for its merits, and not only because of its rank and title.

If we do not arm ourselves with patience, if we do not devote several years to this task, we had better not tackle it at all.

In my opinion we ought to select a minimum number of the higher labor research institutes, etc., which we have baked so hastily, see whether they are organized properly, and allow them to continue working, but only in a way that conforms to the high standards of modern science and gives us all its benefits. If we do that it will not be utopian to hope that within a few years we shall have an institution that will be able to perform its functions, to work systematically and steadily on improving our state apparatus, an institution backed by the trust of the working class, of the Russian Communist Party, and the whole population of our Republic.

The spadework for this could be begun at once. If the People's Commissariat of the Workers' and Peasants' Inspection accepted the present plan of reorganization, it could now take preparatory steps and work methodically until the task is completed, without haste, and not hesitating to alter what has already been done.

Any halfhearted solution would be extremely harmful in this matter. A measure for the size of the staff of the Workers' and Peasants' Inspection based on any other consideration would, in fact, be based on the old bureaucratic considerations, on old prejudices, on what has already been condemned, universally ridiculed, etc.

In substance, the matter is as follows:

Either we prove now that we have really learned something about state organization (we ought to have learned something in five years), or we prove that we are not sufficiently mature for it. If the latter is the case, we had better not tackle the task.

I think that with the available human material it will not be immodest to assume that we have learned enough to be able systematically to rebuild at least one People's Commissariat. True, this one People's Commissariat will have to be the model for our entire state apparatus.

We ought at once to announce a contest in the compilation of two or more textbooks on the organization of labor in general, and on management in particular. We can take as a basis the book already published by Yermansky, although it should be said in parentheses that he obviously sympathizes with Menshevism and is unfit to compile textbooks for the Soviet system. We can also take as a basis the recent book by Kerzhentsev, and some of the other partial textbooks available may be useful too.

We ought to send several qualified and conscientious people to Germany, or to Britain, to collect literature and to study this question. I mention Britain in case it is found impossible to send people to the USA or Canada.

We ought to appoint a commission to draw up the preliminary program of examinations for prospective employees
of the Workers' and Peasants' Inspection; ditto for candidates
to the Central Control Commission.

These and similar measures will not, of course, cause any
difficulties for the People's Commissar or the collegium of
the Workers' and Peasants' Inspection, or for the Presidium
of the Central Control Commission.

Simultaneously, a preparatory commission should be appointed to select candidates for membership of the Central
Control Commission. I hope that we shall now be able to
find more than enough candidates for this post among the
experienced workers in all departments, as well as among
the students of our Soviet higher schools. It would hardly be
right to exclude one or another category beforehand. Probably preference will have to be given to a mixed composition
for this institution, which should combine many qualities,
and dissimilar merits. Consequently, the task of drawing up
the list of candidates will entail a considerable amount of
work. For example, it would be least desirable for the staff
of the new People's Commissariat to consist of people of one
type, only of officials, say, or for it to exclude people of the
propagandist type, or people whose principal quality is
sociability or the ability to penetrate into circles that are not
altogether customary for officials in this field, etc.

I think I shall be able to express my idea best if I compare my plan with that of academic institutions. Under the
guidance of their Presidium, the members of the Central
Control Commission should systematically examine all the
papers and documents of the Political Bureau. Moreover,
they should divide their time correctly between various jobs
in investigating the routine in our institutions, from the very

small and privately owned offices to the highest state institutions. And lastly, their functions should include the study of theory, i.e., the theory of organization of the work they intend to devote themselves to, and practical work under the guidance either of older comrades or of teachers in the higher institutes for the organization of labor.

I do not think, however, that they will be able to confine themselves to this sort of academic work. In addition, they will have to prepare themselves for work which I would not hesitate to call training to catch, I will not say rogues, but something like that, and working out special rules to screen their movements, their approach, etc.

If such proposals were made in West European government institutions they would rouse frightful resentment, a feeling of moral indignation, etc.; but I trust that we have not become so bureaucratic as to be capable of that. NEP has not yet succeeded in gaining such respect as to cause any of us to be shocked at the idea that somebody may be caught. Our Soviet Republic is of such recent construction, and there are such heaps of the old lumber still lying around that it would hardly occur to anyone to be shocked at the idea that we should delve into them by means of ruses, by means of investigations sometimes directed to rather remote sources or in a roundabout way. And even if it did occur to anyone to be shocked by this, we may be sure that such a person would make himself a laughingstock.

Let us hope that our new Workers' and Peasants' Inspection will abandon what the French call *pruderie*, which we may call ridiculous primness, or ridiculous swank, and which plays entirely into the hands of our Soviet and Party bureaucracy. Let it be said in parentheses that we have bureaucrats in our Party offices as well as in Soviet offices.

When I said above that we must study and study hard in

institutes for the higher organization of labor, etc., I did not
by any means imply "studying" in the schoolroom way, nor
did I confine myself to the idea of studying only in the
schoolroom way. I hope that not a single genuine revolutionary will suspect me of refusing, in this case, to understand
"studies" to include resorting to some semihumorous trick,
cunning device, piece of trickery or something of that sort.
I know that in the staid and earnest states of Western Europe
such an idea would horrify people and that not a single decent
official would even entertain it. I hope, however, that we have
not yet become as bureaucratic as all that and that in our
midst the discussion of this idea will give rise to nothing more
than amusement.

Indeed, why not combine pleasure with utility? Why not
resort to some humorous or semihumorous trick to expose
something ridiculous, something harmful, something semi-
ridiculous, semiharmful, etc.?

It seems to me that our Workers' and Peasants' Inspection
will gain a great deal if it undertakes to examine these ideas,
and that the list of cases in which our Central Control Commission and its colleagues in the Workers' and Peasants'
Inspection achieved a few of their most brilliant victories will
be enriched by not a few exploits of our future Workers' and
Peasants' Inspection and Central Control Commission members in places not quite mentionable in prim and staid textbooks.

How can a Party institution be amalgamated with a Soviet
institution? Is there not something improper in this suggestion?

I do not ask these questions on my own behalf, but on

behalf of those I hinted at above when I said that we have bureaucrats in our Party institutions as well as in the Soviet institutions.

But why, indeed, should we not amalgamate the two if this is in the interests of our work? Do we not all see that such an amalgamation has been very beneficial in the case of the People's Commissariat of Foreign Affairs, where it was brought about at the very beginning? Does not the Political Bureau discuss from the Party point of view many questions, both minor and important, concerning the "moves" we should make in reply to the "moves" of foreign powers in order to forestall their, say, cunning, if we are not to use a less respectable term? Is not this flexible amalgamation of a Soviet institution with a Party institution a source of great strength in our politics? I think that what has proved its usefulness, what has been definitely adopted in our foreign politics and has become so customary that it no longer calls forth any doubt in this field, will be at least as appropriate (in fact, I think it will be much more appropriate) for our state apparatus as a whole. The functions of the Workers' and Peasants' Inspection cover our state apparatus as a whole, and its activities should affect all and every state institution without exception: local, central, commercial, purely administrative, educational, archive, theatrical, etc.—in short, all without any exception.

Why then should not an institution, whose activities have such wide scope, and which moreover requires such extraordinary flexibility of forms, be permitted to adopt this peculiar amalgamation of a Party control institution with a Soviet control institution?

I see no obstacles to this. What is more, I think that such an amalgamation is the only guarantee of success in our work. I think that all doubts on this score arise in the dustiest corners of our government offices, and that they deserve to be treated with nothing but ridicule.

Another doubt: is it expedient to combine educational activities with official activities? I think that it is not only expedient, but necessary. Generally speaking, in spite of our revolutionary attitude towards the West European form of state, we have allowed ourselves to become infected with a number of its most harmful and ridiculous prejudices; to some extent we have been deliberately infected with them by our dear bureaucrats, who counted on being able again and again to fish in the muddy waters of these prejudices. And they did fish in these muddy waters to so great an extent that only the blind among us failed to see how extensively this fishing was practiced.

In all spheres of social, economic and political relationships we are "frightfully" revolutionary. But as regards precedence, the observance of the forms and rites of office management, our "revolutionariness" often gives way to the mustiest routine. On more than one occasion, we have witnessed the very interesting phenomenon of a great leap forward in social life being accompanied by amazing timidity whenever the slightest changes are proposed.

This is natural, for the boldest steps forward were taken in a field which was long reserved for theoretical study, which was promoted mainly, and even almost exclusively, in theory. The Russian, when away from work, found solace from bleak bureaucratic realities in unusually bold theoretical constructions, and that is why in our country these unusually bold theoretical constructions assumed an unusually lopsided character. Theoretical audacity in general constructions went hand in hand with amazing timidity as regards certain very minor reforms in office routine. Some great universal agrarian revolution was worked out with an audacity unexampled in any other country, and at the same time the imagination failed when it came to working out a tenth-rate reform in office routine; the imagination, or patience, was lacking to apply to this reform the general propositions that produced such brilliant results when applied to general problems.

That is why in our present life reckless audacity goes hand in hand, to an astonishing degree, with timidity of thought even when it comes to very minor changes.

I think that this has happened in all really great revolutions, for really great revolutions grow out of the contradictions between the old, between what is directed towards developing the old, and the very abstract striving for the new, which must be so new as not to contain the tiniest particle of the old.

And the more abrupt the revolution, the longer will many of these contradictions last.

The general feature of our present life is the following: we have destroyed capitalist industry and have done our best to raze to the ground the medieval institutions and landed proprietorship, and thus created a small and very small peasantry, which is following the lead of the proletariat because it believes in the results of its revolutionary work. It is not easy for us, however, to keep going until the socialist revolution is victorious in more developed countries merely with the aid of this confidence, because economic necessity, especially under NEP, keeps the productivity of labor of the small and very small peasants at an extremely low level. Moreover, the international situation, too, threw Russia back and, by and large, reduced the labor productivity of the people to a level considerably below prewar. The West European capitalist powers, partly deliberately and partly unconsciously, did everything they could to throw us back, to utilize the elements of the Civil War in Russia in order to spread as much ruin in the country as possible. It was precisely this way out of the imperialist war that seemed to have many advantages. They argued somewhat as follows: "If we fail to overthrow the revolutionary system in Russia, we shall, at all events, hinder its progress towards socialism." And from their point of view they could argue in no other way. In the end, their problem was half-solved. They failed to overthrow the new system created by the revolution, but they did prevent it from at once taking the step forward that would have justified the forecasts of the socialists, that would have enabled the latter to develop the productive forces with enormous speed, to develop all the potentialities which, taken together, would have produced socialism; socialists would thus have proved to all and sundry that socialism contains within itself gigantic forces and that mankind had now entered into a new stage of development of extraordinarily brilliant prospects.

The system of international relationships which has now taken shape is one in which a European state, Germany, is enslaved by the victor countries. Furthermore, owing to their victory, a number of states, the oldest states in the West, are in a position to make some insignificant concessions to their oppressed classes—concessions which, insignificant though they are, nevertheless retard the revolutionary movement in those countries and create some semblance of "class truce."

At the same time, as a result of the last imperialist war,

a number of countries of the East, India, China, etc., have been completely jolted out of the rut. Their development has definitely shifted to general European capitalist lines. The general European ferment has begun to affect them, and it is now clear to the whole world that they have been drawn into a process of development that must lead to a crisis in the whole of world capitalism.

Thus, at the present time we are confronted with the question—shall we be able to hold on with our small and very small peasant production, and in our present state of ruin, until the West European capitalist countries consummate their development towards socialism? But they are consummating it not as we formerly expected. They are not consummating it through the gradual "maturing" of socialism, but through the exploitation of some countries by others, through the exploitation of the first of the countries vanquished in the imperialist war combined with the exploitation of the whole of the East. On the other hand, precisely as a result of the first imperialist war, the East has been definitely drawn into the revolutionary movement, has been definitely drawn into the general maelstrom of the world revolutionary movement.

What tactics does this situation prescribe for our country? Obviously the following. We must display extreme caution so as to preserve our workers' government and to retain our small and very small peasantry under its leadership and authority. We have the advantage that the whole world is now passing to a movement that must give rise to a world socialist revolution. But we are laboring under the disadvantage that the imperialists have succeeded in splitting the world into two camps; and this split is made more complicated by the fact that it is extremely difficult for Germany, which is really a land of advanced, cultured, capitalist development, to rise to her feet. All the capitalist powers of what is called the West are pecking at her and preventing her from rising. On the other hand, the entire East, with its hundreds of millions of exploited working people, reduced to the last degree of human suffering, has been forced into a position where its physical and material strength cannot possibly be compared with the physical, material and military strength of any of the much smaller West European states.

Can we save ourselves from the impending conflict with these imperialist countries? May we hope that the internal antagonisms and conflicts between the thriving imperialist countries of the West and the thriving imperialist countries of the East will give us a second respite as they did the first time, when the campaign of the West European counterrevolution in support of the Russian counterrevolution broke down owing to the antagonisms in the camp of the counterrevolutionaries of West and the East, in the camp of the Eastern and Western exploiters, in the camp of Japan and the USA?

I think the reply to this question should be that the issue depends upon too many factors, and that the outcome of the struggle as a whole can be forecast only because in the long run capitalism itself is educating and training the vast majority of the population of the globe for the struggle.

In the last analysis, the outcome of the struggle will be determined by the fact that Russia, India, China, etc., account for the overwhelming majority of the population of the globe. And during the past few years it is this majority that has been drawn into the struggle for emancipation with extraordinary rapidity, so that in this respect there cannot be the slightest doubt what the final outcome of the world struggle will be. In this sense, the complete victory of socialism is fully and absolutely assured.

But what interests us is not the inevitability of this complete victory of socialism, but the tactics which we, the Russian Communist Party, we, the Russian Soviet Government, should pursue to prevent the West European counter-revolutionary states from crushing us. To ensure our existence until the next military conflict between the counter-revolutionary imperialist West and the revolutionary and nationalist East, between the most civilized countries of the world and the Orientally backward countries which, however, comprise the majority, this majority must become civilized. We, too, lack enough civilization to enable us to pass straight on to socialism, although we do have the political requisites for it. We should adopt the following tactics, or pursue the following policy, to save ourselves.

We must strive to build up a state in which the workers retain the leadership of the peasants, in which they retain the confidence of the peasants, and by exercising the greatest economy remove every trace of extravagance from our social relations.

We must reduce our state apparatus to the utmost degree of economy. We must banish from it all traces of extravagance, of which so much has been left over from tsarist Russia, from its bureaucratic capitalist state machine.

Will not this be a reign of peasant limitations?

No. If we see to it that the working class retains its leadership over the peasantry, we shall be able, by exercising the greatest possible thrift in the economic life of our state, to use every saving we make to develop our large-scale machine industry, to develop electrification, the hydraulic extraction of peat, to complete the Volkhov Power Project, etc.

In this, and in this alone, lies our hope. Only when we have done this shall we, speaking figuratively, be able to change horses, to change from the peasant, muzhik horse of poverty, from the horse of an economy designed for a ruined peasant country, to the horse which the proletariat is seeking and must seek—the horse of large-scale machine industry, of electrification, of the Volkhov Power Station, etc.

That is how I link up in my mind the general plan of our work, of our policy, of our tactics, of our strategy, with the functions of the reorganized Workers' and Peasants' Inspection. This is what, in my opinion, justifies the exceptional care, the exceptional attention that we must devote to the Workers' and Peasants' Inspection in raising it to an exceptionally high level, in giving it a leadership with Central Committee rights, etc., etc.

And this justification is that only by thoroughly purging our government machine, by reducing to the utmost everything that is not absolutely essential in it, shall we be certain of being able to keep going. Moreover, we shall be able to keep going not on the level of a small-peasant country, not on the level of universal limitation, but on a level steadily advancing to large-scale machine industry.

These are the lofty tasks that I dream of for our Workers' and Peasants' Inspection. That is why I am planning for it the amalgamation of the most authoritative Party body with an "ordinary" People's Commissariat.

March 2, 1923

[English translation: V. I. Lenin, *Collected Works,* 4th ed. (Moscow, Progress Publishers, 1960–   ), Vol. XXXIII, pp. 487–502. Source: *Soch.,* Vol. XLV, pp. 387–406]

X

NOTE ON LENIN'S ILLNESS
AFTER MARCH 10, 1923

The paralysis of the right side of the body and the loss of speech that occurred on March 10 seemed so alarming that the government decided to reveal the seriousness of the illness. From then on *Izvestia* published a daily health bulletin. On May 15, Lenin was moved from his apartment in the Kremlin to his country house at Gorki. Two months later, in July, a miracle seems to have occurred: Lenin's health began to improve again. He began to take walks and to practice writing with his left hand. He was even able to visit the chairman of the local *sovkhoz* and spend three days with him.

About August 10 he was allowed to write. He received *Pravda* every day and later *Izvestia* and other publications. Before long he was able to read books and had a reading list drawn up for him. It was usually Krupskaya who read him newspaper articles and perhaps passages from the books he asked for; he was far from completely cured. It was all the more astonishing that he managed to get permission for the journey he undertook on October 18. He traveled to Moscow, went to the Kremlin by car, then set off again to wander the streets and to visit the Agricultural Exhibition. He then went back to his office, remained silent for a long time, took out some books from his library and returned to Gorki.

Between November 24 and December 16, Bukharin, Preobrazhensky, Skvortsov-Stepanov, Krestinsky, Pyatnitsky and the editor of the *Krasnaya Nov*, Voronsky, came to see him. They talked to him about current affairs and brought news that Lenin listened to attentively, but he does not seem to have recovered the use of speech—the chronology contained in Volume XLV of the *Sochineniya,* which mentions the loss of speech, does not return to the matter again.

At the beginning of 1924 Lenin attended a Christmas party organized at the *sovkhoz.* On January 19, in a sledge, he followed a hunting expedition in the forest. But between January 17 and 20 his time was mainly taken up with reading the report of the Thirteenth Party Congress. Lenin appeared very attentive and sometimes asked questions by gestures; certain points quite obviously irritated him, but Krupskaya managed to calm him, probably by inventing information for the purpose.

On January 21, 1924, Lenin's health suddenly deteriorated. He died at 6:50 P.M.

BIOGRAPHICAL
NOTES

BUKHARIN, N. I. (1888–1938): Outstanding leader and theoretician of the Bolshevik Party, candidate member of the Politburo at Lenin's death, later full member, leader of the so-called "Right Opposition" in 1928–1929. Executed after the third Moscow trial in 1938.

DZERZHINSKY, F. E. (1877–1926): Important party leader, head of the political police, of interior affairs, and Commissar of Railroads and Communications.

FOTIEVA, L. A. (1881–   ): Party member since 1904, Secretary of the Sovnarkom and Lenin's private secretary.

GORBUNOV, N. P. (1892–1938): Head of the Sovnarkom secretariat and thus, practically, Lenin's administrative aid. Perished in Stalin's purges.

KAMENEV, L. B. (1883–1936): Important party leader, opposed to Lenin's *coup d'état* in 1917, but soon reconciled himself with Lenin, became Politburo member and one of Lenin's three deputies in the Sovnarkom. After Lenin's death, one of the ruling trio (with Zinoviev and Stalin) but turned against Stalin in 1925 and soon lost leading position. Executed after the Moscow trial in 1936.

---

[1] The purpose of this brief listing is to provide biographical data on some of the less well known personalities mentioned in the text. Thus there are no entries for Lenin, Trotsky and Stalin. The data has also been restricted on the whole to that part of a given individual's career coincident with the events of this book.

178 LENIN'S LAST STRUGGLE

KAPSUKAS-MITSKEVITCHIUS, V. S. (1882–   ): Party member of Lithuanian origin, member of the committee of inquiry, headed by Dzerzhinsky, sent to Georgia by the Politburo.

KRESTINSKY, N. N. (1883–1938): Old Bolshevik, Secretary of the Central Committee from December 1919 till March 1921. Later Soviet ambassador in Germany. In 1930, Deputy Commissar of Foreign Affairs. Perished in the purges of the thirties.

KRUPSKAYA, N. K. (1869–1939): Lenin's wife and collaborator.

KRZHIZHANOVSKY, G. M. (1872–1959): Party member, engineer, and scholar. Headed the Gosplan in 1921–1930.

KUIBYSHEV, V. V. (1888–1935): Party leader, army commissar in Turkestan during the civil war, became Secretary of the Central Committee when Stalin took over the Party secretariat in April 1922. Headed later the CCC-RKI, the VSNKH, the Gosplan and other posts. Member of the Politburo since 1927.

MAKHARADZE, F. I. (1886–1925): Important Bolshevik leader in Georgia, president of the Georgian TSIK, member of the Caucasian Party Bureau.

MDIVANI, P. G. (1887–1937): Georgian revolutionary, Old Bolshevik, civil-war commissar, member of the Caucasian Bureau of the CC and of the CC of the Georgian Communist Party until the collective resignation of this Committee in October 1922 because of their opposition to Stalin's policies on the national question. Soviet commercial representative in France from 1924, deputy chairman of the Georgian government from 1931 to 1936. Later purged.

MILYUTIN, V. P. (1884–1938): Old Bolshevik, one of the first leaders of the VSNKH.

MOLOTOV, V. M. (1890–   ): In the Bolshevik Party since 1906, important Party leader till his demotion by N. S. Khrushchev, was elected to the CC in 1911 and then became Secretary of the CC and deputy member of the Politburo.

ORDZHONIKIDZE, G. K. (1886–1937): Old Bolshevik, Georgian, the Party's military and administrative leader in the Caucasus during the civil war and the Party's plenipotentiary there until 1926 when he took over the CCC-RKI. He rose to the CC in 1921, and to the Politburo in 1930. From 1930 onwards he was head of the country's heavy industry until his suicide in 1937.

PETROVSKY, G. I. (1878–1958): Old Party member. President of the Ukrainian TSIK from 1919 to 1939, and member of the Party's CC.

PREOBRAZHENSKY, E. A. (1886–1937): Old Party member, economist, Secretary of the Party's CC 1920–1921. He was expelled from the Party in 1927 for Trotskyism, later readmitted, but finally perished during the purges.

PYATAKOV, G. L. (1890–1937): Important leader, economist, recommended by Lenin for the post of deputy chairman of the Gosplan. Excluded in 1927 for Trotskyism, readmitted in 1928. He was Ordzhonikidze's deputy in the commissariat of heavy industry. Perished in the purges.

RADEK, K. B. (1885–1939): Member of the Polish and German Social Democratic parties, he joined the Bolsheviks in 1917. Important leader of the Komintern, able speaker and writer. Expelled for Trotskyism in 1927, readmitted in 1929, sentenced to imprisonment in 1936.

RAKOVSKY, K. G. (1873–1941): A Bulgarian socialist, joined the Bolsheviks in 1917, headed the Ukrainian Sovnarkom in 1918–1923. Ambassador in Paris and London, expelled from the Party in 1927 for Trotskyism, readmitted in 1935, but arrested and sent to camp in 1938.

RYKOV, A. I. (1881–1938): Important party leader, headed the VSNKH from 1918 to 1921, and was later Lenin's deputy in the Sovnarkom and STO. Lenin's heir as head of Sovnarkom until 1930, he turned against Stalin as leader of the "Right Opposition" from 1928. Executed after a show trial in 1938.

SKVORTSOV-STEPANOV, I. I. (1870–1928): A Party scholar and minor political leader. Translated Marx's *Capital* into Russian, and headed the Lenin Institute after Lenin's death.

SOKOLNIKOV, G. YA. (1888–1939): Old Party member who held important posts in Soviet diplomacy and economic administration. Commissar of Finances 1922–1926. Victim of the purges.

SOLTZ, A. A. (1872–1945): Old Party member. Member of the CCC leading caucus and of the Supreme Court from 1921.

SEREBRYAKOV, L. P. (1890–   ): Old Bolshevik of Trotskyite leanings, was Secretary of the Party's CC 1919–1920, together with Preobrazhensky and Krestinsky.

TOMSKY, M. P. (1880–1936): In the Party since 1904. Head of the Soviet trade unions till his ouster in 1928 as one of the leaders of the "rightist deviation." Member of the Politburo since 1922. Executed after trial in 1936.

TSYURUPA, A. D. (1870–1928): Old Bolshevik, Commissar of Supplies, 1918–1921. Lenin's deputy in the Sovnarkom from the end of 1921. Member of the CC.

ULYANOVA, M. I. (1878–1937): Lenin's sister. She worked on the board of *Pravda,* but otherwise did not play any conspicuous role.

VOLODICHEVA, M. A.: Lenin's private secretary. He charged her, together with Fotieva and Gorbunov, with the task of secretly investigating the Georgian affair.

ZINOVIEV, G. E. (1883–1936): Important Bolshevik leader. He and Kamenev opposed both Lenin's *coup d'état* and his intentions to form a strictly Bolshevik government. Member of the Politburo under Lenin and leader of the Komintern, he joined with Kamenev and Stalin against Trotsky after Lenin's death, but in 1925 turned against Stalin and allied himself with Trotsky. After that he was frequently expelled and readmitted to the Party, but was definitely ousted from leadership. He was executed after the first Moscow trial in 1936.

INDEX

bureaucracy (*cont.*)
initiated by dictatorship of Party, 16; should first be eliminated from leadership, 67; hardly affected by Soviet spirit, 86; Lenin suspicious of, 92; its entrenchment in Soviet system, 124ff.; *see also* civil servants, *chinovnichestvo*
businessmen, *xiv*, 23–24, 36, 133
Byelorussia, 43, 47, 54, 145, 150

cadres, *xiv*, 5, 13, 17, 123
Canada, 163
Carr, E. H., 16, 125
Caucasian Bureau of CP (*Kavburo*): given job of economic unification of the three Caucasian Republics, 44; regional leadership renamed *Zakkraykom*, 44; *see* Transcaucasian Federation
Caucasian Republics, 44, 45; *see also* national Republics, individual Republics by name
Central Committee (*Tseka*), 12, 32, 36–37, 44–46, 49, 51, 53–54, 56, 78, 79, 84, 93, 118–19, 132; *see also* tsekisty
Central Control Commission, 71, 130, 132, 161, 164, 166; Lenin proposes to

merge with Workers' and Peasants' Inspection, 93; had report on Ordzhonikidze incident which disappeared, 97; to be increased in size, 119; would devote part of its time to study of management control, 121; under Stalin, 128; problem of guaranteeing independence of new CCC-RKI, 126–27; new CCC-RKI would educate the *tsekisty*, 131
centralism: imperative in face of White armies, 12; unsanctioned by theory, 13; not "egocentralism," 15; and internationalism, 62
Cheka, 29, 134
Cherviakov, representative for Byelorussia, 47, 49
China, 106, 110, 171, 172; communes of, *ix*
chinovnichestvo, chinovniki, 8, 9, 120, 126; *see also* bureaucracy, civil servants
civil servants, 118; census of, 92–93
civil war, 4–5, 12, 32
Commissar: for the Nationalities (Stalin), 15, 47; for Workers' and Peasants' Inspection (Stalin), 15, 120
Commissariat: of Foreign Affairs, 167; of Foreign Trade, 35, 152; of Workers' and Peasants' Inspection (RKI),

Printed and bound by CPI Group (UK) Ltd, Croydon, CR0 4YY

09/06/2025

14686118-0001